Wesley's Wars is a rich treasury of insight into Wesleyan thought and practice that is written to be accessible to the average reader and yet substantial enough To engage those who consider themselves Wesleyan scholars. It opens a new door to understanding the complexity and practicality of John Wesley's thought and practice. It is a work clearly focused on those who consider themselves Wesleyan but will also prove accessible and helpful to the ecumenical community. I commend it to all who desire to grow in their knowledge and practice of the Christian fa⋅

Bishop R
Retired

J. Robert Ewbank brings John Wesley to life draws us not only to Wesley the theologian-preacher but equally important to Wesley the man. As a professor of philosophy, I was particularly intrigued by the way Wesley was a man who understood the currents of his time and the spirit of his age. Ewbank carefully interlaces the way Wesley set the pace for battles of doctrinal purity. This was a revelation to me to see how Wesley leveraged the battle for biblical truth into the larger plane of the battleground we inherit today.

Years of seminary gave me a general introduction to the life of Wesley and the way he changed his world and ours. But for me this book was a journey into the mind of a man I knew only as a man, a great man, but still a stranger to me. Now, having read this book I feel I was treated to a case study of a man who cared, loved, thought and engaged his world. I had no idea of the depth of Wesley's thinking and scope of his writings.

For the first time I feel like I've begun to grasp Wesley's disagreements with Predestination. Ewbank, via Wesley's writings, breaks it down to its basic components showing the way Wesley's mind worked without the need for theological entanglement and sometimes confusing jargon. More than that, this book revealed Wesley's uncommon courage to stand against even supporters who turned on him labeling him as a heretic. It's easy to feel camaraderie with a man like that. For me, it was the drama in the background that kept me engaged with the theological disputes. It was a strange feeling of connection across the centuries, brother to brother.

This book is more than another expose on the life and teaching of John Wesley. It's an inspirational inroad into the mind of a man whose life transcends the seasons that lie between us.

Terry Bell
Sr. Pastor, Life Park Christian Fellowship

WESLEY'S WARS
(THEOLOGICAL)

J. ROBERT EWBANK

ALSO BY J. ROBERT EWBANK
JOHN WESLEY, NATURAL MAN, AND THE 'ISMS'

WESTBOW
PRESS
A DIVISION OF THOMAS NELSON

WestBow Press books may be ordered through booksellers or by contacting:

WestBow Press
A Division of Thomas Nelson
1663 Liberty Drive
Bloomington, IN 47403
www.westbowpress.com
1-(866) 928-1240

Because of the dynamic nature of the Internet, any web addresses or links contained in this book may have changed since publication and may no longer be valid. The views expressed in this work are solely those of the author and do not necessarily reflect the views of the publisher, and the publisher hereby disclaims any responsibility for them.

Any people depicted in stock imagery provided by Thinkstock are models, and such images are being used for illustrative purposes only.

Certain stock imagery © Thinkstock.

ISBN: 978-1-4497-4398-7 (sc)

Library of Congress Control Number: 2012905266

Printed in the United States of America

WestBow Press rev. date: 05/02/2012

To William Hordern who taught me to love theology,
To Colin Williams who taught me to love John Wesley's theology,
To Philip S. Watson who led my advanced study of Wesley's theology,
To my wife who supported and encouraged me,
Thanks

CONTENTS

PREFACE

This book is a work of love for the theology of John Wesley. Wesley is one of the true religious genius's that the world has ever seen. He and his brother accounted for around 500 publications, most written or edited by John. He rode thousands of miles on horseback and preached an average, it is said, of three sermons a day, all while being responsible for the religious life of those who were members of his society which became the Methodist Church.

This book is not written exclusively about the core of his theology which is the order of salvation. It is a book about those vital theological issues that he dealt with in his ministry.

The key thing to remember about Wesley and his works is that he was forever looking out for the religious good of those members in his society. He believed in Christianity, and that which he found within the Church of England with all his heart. Of course he differed with many who interpreted the theology found there, but he found within its teachings the source or at least confirmation of his theological beliefs within that Church.

It is exciting to look at the wars which he entered into and to think of those he fought against, and how these wars affected his societies and their religious health.

The doctrines he fought for include some which are normal, but a few are somewhat unusual or out of the ordinary. For instance, original sin, the means of grace, and the doctrine of the church are not unusual. However, his doctrines of prevenient grace and perfection though found elsewhere within Christianity are certainly not commonly proclaimed, then or now. His perception of the church universal is unusual in a person of his time for its extreme ecumenicity.

Agree or disagree with him, he is always logical, perceptive, straight forward, and usually courteous to his opponents, almost to a fault.

ACKNOWLEDGEMENTS

This book, just like any other, could not have been written without the help and encouragement of many others.

My parents played a large part in their encouragement of my activities. John R. Ewbank, was a second generation Methodist Minister and college professor. Mattie Ewbank was a teacher and profound helper and guide to me.

No one succeeds without some teachers they met along the way. Those who particularly played a part in this creation came from Garrett Evangelical Theological Seminary, Evanston, Illinois. Dr. William Hordern taught me to love the study of theology and Dr. Colin Williams taught and inspired me to love the theology of John Wesley. Special thanks must go to Philip S. Watson, counselor without peer, who worked with me on the theology of John Wesley when I returned to Garrett after graduating with my Master's Degree to work on another Master's Degree in the theology of John Wesley. It is with deep regret that I was unable to finish that program.

My two encouraging spouses made sure that I did not give up but continued to work. Three children also contributed, Glenda Sealy, Shawn R. Ewbank and Todd C. Ewbank. Through my wife I have also come to know her son, Rob Brandon.

Undoubtedly I have missed many others. Sorry to have not singled you out, but you are appreciated.

INTRODUCTION

Some may think Wesley's theology is out of date and is therefore no longer applicable to us moderns. Since he wrote in the 18th century some may think he obviously has nothing to offer our advanced age.

Wesley faces some of the same or similar problems we face today. The condition of man has not changed at all, at least in his relationship with God and with his fellow man.

Robert G. Tuttle in his introduction to Philip S. Watson's book "Anatomy of a Conversion" says it so well.

> Professor Watson states in his Introduction, "There is not much that is new fundamentally new—under the sun." The longer I live the more sense that statement makes to me. Today people still need to be saved; the Wesleys speak to that. Today people still need to fear sin as much as death or hell; the Wesleys speak to that. Today people still oppress each other; the Wesleys speak to that. Today the church still needs fellowship and accountability; the Wesleys speak to that. Today love is still the beginning and end of the Christian faith; the Wesleys speak to that—and so much, much more![1]

John Wesley was involved in several theological wars during his lifetime. Some of these were very protracted and lasted pretty much throughout his career but some were of shorter term and often the initial clash may not have been forgotten but at least it did not consume as much of his attention.

Most of these wars were engaged in by Wesley because he thought Christianity itself hung in the balance between the two views. If the opposing view was successful Christianity as he knew and believed it would be seriously damaged or destroyed.

---

[1] Watson, Philip S., *Anatomy of a Conversion*, x

Some of these wars were particularly painful for Wesley because they involved issues which were within and divided Methodism itself. Regardless of the reason, Wesley saw these particular issues as important enough for him to do battle. We will discuss these issues which were of enough interest to him, that he felt called upon to respond to them.

It is difficult or almost impossible to understand Wesley and his theology unless we are aware of a few facts about him and his life. These facts undoubtedly shape his thought and go a long way in determining its presentation.

He is primarily a preacher, minister, educator, church organizer, and builder. After all, he preached about 42,000 sermons, he and his brother wrote and edited around 500 titles with John writing and editing the bulk of them, and he rode about 250,000 miles on horseback or carriage during his career. These are not the normal activities of what we today, or for them for that matter, would consider normal for a theologian. Fancy any living theologian trying to do the equivalent today.

John Wesley's theology is developed from and addressed to his situation as a pastor and leader of a society. He preaches to those who are not attending a church as well as those who are under churched. He often even preaches in the open air, outside without benefit of pulpit, pews, roofs, or altars. He preaches to bring salvation to them so they can meet the God he has already met. Not only does he wish to bring them to salvation (justification) he wants even more to bring them to the full Christian life with God (sanctification, or Christian perfection) if that is possible. The extreme difference between these two doctrines and the significance of each of them for the Christian life will be discussed later.

Naturally most of his time is devoted to being the spiritual leader of those who have accepted him as such. In this role he does find it mandatory to protect and defend the faith of his followers from the ideas or utter mistakes of some Christian thinkers, or really theological errors presented by these thinkers, which are capable of misleading his followers.

Wesley builds his theology around the order of salvation. To understand Wesley's approach we must remember his focus on pastoral concerns for his followers and how he can best care for them. His pastoral concerns do not lend themselves to developing a full blown theology because it was not needed. You will not find a structured, reasoned, theology of the Trinity, or of Christ being both human and divine (Incarnation) in Wesley. Those are interesting theological concepts but not the type of sermon or theological formulation required to get people into heaven or heaven into people. As a preacher trying to introduce his congregation to Christ and thereby seeking their salvation, some doctrines are obviously more important than others. He did believe in the doctrines of the Trinity and the Incarnation and there is plenty of evidence in his writings to show the truth of this statement. However, doctrines such as these are not the focus of his life, preaching, or his writings.

His theology of salvation is not a simple one either. It is a very complex theology which pulls together themes which many would say are not compatible but he somehow found a way to put them together in a dynamic tension. Kenneth J. Collins calls it a theology with "tensions and conjunctions."[2] The same concept but called "balance" and "both/and" is found in the work of Paul Wesley Chilcote: "Even more importantly, Wesleyan theology has an important contribution to make to contemporary Christianity as a whole. It is a 'both/and' rather than an 'either/or' theology, a bridge-building tradition that can speak with alacrity and healing to an age of serious division in God's family."[3]

The theology of Wesley is found in his published Sermons, Works, Notes on the Bible—particularly the New Testament—with some to be found in the Letters and Journals. His life's occupation pretty much forces him to use these methods of communicating his thought. Occasionally he would deem a situation or problem so compelling he would write a tract to cover the issue. Most of these writings are found in the Works.

Wesley's theology is predominantly found in his sermons with occasional trips to the Works for longer presentations involving his wars. The Sermons are pretty comprehensive, at least in the area of his greatest interest which is the order of salvation. Again, as we know, the order of salvation is the heart of Wesley's theology.

The Sermons and Notes were written to be the standard in theological thought for his preachers and his followers. Though they are called sermons, and many were preached by Wesley, some seem to have been written for

---

2 Collins, *The Scripture Way of Salvation*, 16
3 Chilcote, *Recapturing the Wesley's Vision*, 11

Methodists to understand their theology. No modern preacher would try to preach Wesley's sermons from the pulpit today in the form we have them. Perhaps some of them were written to be read rather than to be preached, however styles of preaching have changed over the years. The English Methodist Church requires their ministers to read and follow the thinking of the Standard Sermons and the Notes—or at least not contradict them.

Because of his life's work it should not come as a great surprise to find that John is a practical, rather than systematic, theologian. This fact should not be surprising due to his career which we have just discussed. Systematic theologians today may write volumes of books in which they have neatly separated into chapters the doctrines they are discussing. This makes for easier reading by us, except naturally, for any technical language they may use. This neat separation and division into theological concepts is great for us to see how a particular person's theology fits together or how the various parts or elements mesh to form a neat whole. It is also easy for the reader to find a particular doctrine and read only about the specific doctrine or doctrines they are seeking to study.

Some may not want to pursue the study of Wesley because his theology is not written in neat volumes of systematic theology. If one were to skip reading Wesley for this reason it would be a tragic mistake. We would then miss some important and significant contributions Wesley has made to Christian theology.

It is impossible to study Wesley without at least being aware of his brother Charles's contribution to John's thought and his work. Charles supported his brother in most of his theological battles and the poetic results are found in the Wesley Hymnbook and in the poetic works of Charles Wesley.

Wesley's theological wars will be discussed by looking at the ideas or concepts he is warring against. Sometimes these ideas or concepts come from a particular person but sometimes they come from a group or many people with similar concepts. We will also look at how Wesley handles his attack or response as he defends Christianity.

The first war we will discuss concerns the doctrine of original sin and how important it is for Christianity. We will find this doctrine is basic for an understanding of Christian theology.

Dr. John Taylor, in his book which we will discuss in that chapter, puts forth a deistic concept of the doctrine of original sin. His thought is not so far removed from some of the humanistic and puffed up thinking we today have about man and his place in the universe. Man has successfully found ways to replace God with himself during all ages, so it is not surprising to find he is doing it today.

Taylor's reduction of original sin to almost a meaningless concept is for most Christians totally inadequate and unacceptable. It does not do justice to the concept of original sin nor does it have the more compelling and deeper understanding of man and his relationship to God and his fellow man which the more orthodox presentation gives.

Wesley places a significant importance upon this doctrine which is shown in two respects. The first is he takes the time to defend it and the second is in how he defends it. Wesley does not engage in a battle every time he disagrees with somebody's thinking. When he does decide to do battle it is important to him. In this particular case he takes great care and a lot of time in making his defense of the doctrine of original sin.

Truly this is a doctrine we must come to grips with today if we are going to understand the heights and depths of the Christian faith. We do not like to talk about sin today, particularly our own sins which we tend to omit, misclassify, explain away, or deny altogether.

Our attention will then turn to Wesley's long war with the then current Calvinistic doctrine of predestination. We will do so by examining his doctrine of prevenient or preventing grace which is the perfect and probably only antidote to predestination.

Wesley can come within a hair's breadth of Calvin in describing the condition of man in his relationship with God and yet he is able to avoid the twin elements of predestination—election and reprobation. Calvin's doctrine of predestination is that from the foundation of the world God determined who were going to be saved (election) and those who were to be damned (reprobation).

Wesley found many reasons to avoid the doctrine of predestination. In fact he found the doctrine to be repugnant and very dangerous for the Christian. As a proponent of holiness and the full Christian life, he thought the doctrine of predestination managed to short circuit them and thereby lead the followers of predestination astray. The holiness of life was likely to be downplayed, if not almost forgotten altogether by those who believe in predestination.

The concept of predestination warred against the full Christian life of holiness. This life of Christian holiness is man's accepting God's grace which is given over and over if man accepts it, and then how man works out his own salvation with God.

The next battle involves the Moravians who taught Wesley many good things but who also appeared to him to be lacking in some very important areas.

This war was fought on several fronts and involved the definition of good works, a Christian life of holiness, and the use of the means of grace.

A couple of key questions arise in this discussion. The first involves the Christian faith and the question asked is the Christian faith better to be described as a growth process or as a faith once given and is therefore complete?

The second involves the question of how one waits or prepares for the Christian life. Are we to wait quietly, without actions on our part which could be construed as human works for our salvation, or are we to use all of the means of grace God has provided us which are not considered as works of man for salvation, because it is God's grace which is given first and which we then accept or reject?

Our discussion then turns to Wesley and the Church of England, the Anglican Church. Though John was a minister in that church his entire life he was often accused of leaving the Church of England and taking the Methodists with him.

He had a rocky relationship with the church and many of the ministers within the church. By his own account he was most often a dutiful son of the church. This complex relationship will be discussed. The definition of the church is a focus of this war.

The doctrine of Christian perfection is responsible for one of the great theological wars which Wesley wages.

Wesley was attacked from all sides on this one. There were those who believed justification and sanctification were the same, who thought he made Christian perfection too high and believe it or not, those who thought it was defined as too low. He had to defend his thought on Christian perfection against all of them.

There were those who saw some abuses with the term perfection itself. Wesley saw these abuses also and was wary of them. There were those who did not see or understand Wesley's emphasis upon holiness of life and the importance of seeking Christian perfection in this life.

We will finish our thinking together about Wesley's theology with a short chapter on some of the ways in which Wesley was an ecumenical thinker and theologian. I have expressed some of these ideas before but some are new and they are put forward to allow Wesley to speak to us of the love we are to have for one another in our Christian brotherhood. If only we today were wise enough to read and follow Wesley on these points!

1

ORIGINAL SIN

A. INTRODUCTION

The first of John Wesley's theological wars we will discuss is the one he waged on behalf of the Doctrine of original sin. Wesley normally does not become engaged in a theological war unless he believes Christianity is attacked in a way he thinks will destroy real Christianity if the opposing position is allowed to stand victorious. Certainly the doctrine of original sin and the theological war waged against it by Dr. John Taylor is one of this magnitude and Wesley responds in a way that marks the importance of this battle.

The opening salvo of this theological war begins in 1740 with the publishing of "The Scripture-Doctrine of Original Sin, Exposed to Free and Candid Examination," written by Dr. John Taylor of Norwich (1694-1761).

This was an outstanding time for books written on the doctrine of original sin because two other books on the identical topic were published the same year. These two books were written from a different perspective than Taylor's and are much more in line with Wesley's thinking but they apparently do not get as much play or readership as Taylor's. The times and common humanistic background which are current in the thinking of the age argue against a more classic presentation of original sin. It does, however, welcome very well a book which presents the progress of humanity and the reduction of the seriousness of sin.

The other two books published in 1740 on the topic are "The Ruin and Recovery of Mankind" by Isaac Watts and "A Vindication of the

Scripture-Doctrine of Original Sin" by David Jennings. Since two books were published in favor of a more classic interpretation of original sin to only one against that view, one might think the classic interpretation could claim the day and the victory. If it had happened that way we would not be able to read Wesley's defense of the doctrine of original sin, and there would be no reason for this chapter.

The mere publishing of a book which Wesley did not care for would certainly not be enough to bring him to the battle. Many books printed were published with which Wesley did not agree, but they did not call him forth to produce a defense of Christianity. The difference is, Taylor's book enjoys a better reading than the other two books, and in fact it enjoys a great readership even in the seminaries of the time where the future ministers of the Church of England are being trained. Wesley says one of the current Church Fathers is even quoted as saying he can think of no better book than Taylor's to give to young clergymen. It is more likely this event was the catalyst, the infecting of the seminaries with Dr. Taylor's thought, and its being taught to future ministers which eventually brings Wesley into the fray. He finally responds, and when he does there are no captives taken and no punches pulled. Wesley is on a mission for the preservation of Christianity.

Wesley believes the book by Taylor is getting way too much attention and acceptance among academic circles and no one has taken on the project of adequately answering the deistic challenge to the doctrine of original sin which Taylor's book represents.

Wesley does not begin to write until 1756, sixteen years after the publication of Taylor's book. Apparently no one in Wesley's mind has properly defended Christianity from this deistic challenge. As he prepares his answers to Taylor Wesley finds some other resources he perhaps is unaware of before beginning his defense of the doctrine of original sin. If he was aware of them he apparently did not believe they adequately answered the challenge Taylor has brought.

In his preface Wesley compliments Dr. Taylor in many ways. Some of these compliments are made to show the reader how easy it is for one to read Taylor's book and be misled about the true meaning of the doctrine of original sin.

> The author is doubtless a person of sense, nay, of unusually strong understanding, joined with no small liveliness of imagination, and a good degree of various learning. He has likewise an admirable command of temper, so that he almost everywhere speaks as one in good humour. Add to this, that he has a smooth and pleasing, yet a manly and nervous, style. And all these talents he exerts to the uttermost, on a favourite subject, in the Treatise before us; which he has had leisure for many years to revise, file, correct, and strengthen against all objections.[1]

He finds it difficult to understand why some of the educated and trained people of the age have not taken on the job of correcting the deistic errors of Taylor's thesis. Wesley had hoped others would take on the project of showing the false doctrinal presentations of Taylor and support the more classical concepts of original sin. Wesley does not find adequately expressed the support he thinks necessary to win this particular theological war. At least he does not think anyone yet has adequately defended the Christian faith from this error. Tragically, no one has risen to war effectively against the deistic challenge of Taylor, so Wesley has to venture forth alone.

In his preface Wesley points out that Taylor's book is really a presentation of deism against Christianity.

> . . . it may be doubted whether the scheme before us be not far more dangerous than open Deism itself. It does not shock us like barefaced infidelity: We feel no pain, and suspect no evil, while it steals like "water into our bowels," like "oil into our bones." One who would be upon his guard in reading the works of Dr. Middleton, or Lord Bolingbroke, is quite open and unguarded in reading the smooth, decent writings of Dr. Taylor; one who does not oppose, (far be it from him!) but only explain, the Scripture; who does not raise any difficulties or objections against the Christian Revelation, but only removes those with which it had been unhappily encumbered for so many centuries![2]

---

[1] Wesley, *Works*, 9:192

[2] Wesley, *Works*, 9:193

The deistic challenge so ably and effectively presented by Taylor is a reduction of original sin and the consequences of original sin. The problem for Wesley and any theologian who is closer to the classical or orthodox presentation of the doctrine of original sin is if sin is reduced to something which is of no or little consequence then the work God performed through His Son on the cross is of no or little consequence. In other words, if the cross is theologically required to provide the answer to the sin of man and the sin of man is reduced to something which is not very important, then the work God performed through the cross is not very important either. These two doctrines (sin and salvation) rise or fall together in importance. Minimizing one minimizes the other; strengthening or heightening one does the same to the other.

The minimizing of sin reduces the impact of the rest of Christianity as well. If sin is a "whoopsie" or a "slipper's don't count," or a small error, then the cross, justification, new birth and sanctification become of little consequence as well. If, according to the positive and humanistic outlook of the day, we are capable of and indeed are getting better every day; if we are pretty well or are well at least in a religious sense we have little reason for a savior, then there is nothing from which to save us.

We now see the extreme importance of what one thinks about original sin because it is the foundation for our further theological thoughts. This doctrine affects them all. The particular concept one has of original sin determines how consequential the other doctrines are going to be within Christianity. The crux of theology thus becomes the doctrine of sin because everything else relates to this single doctrine. If there is no such thing as sin there is no need for the rest of the Christian doctrines.

Wesley believes if we reduce the doctrine of original sin and its consequences in this way we are striking at the root of Christianity and he will not allow this blow to be struck—not on his watch.

Wesley points out the supposition of Taylor's book: we humans are spiritually well, and because we are spiritually well we have no need of a physician. To put it another way, if Taylor's thesis is correct and he presents the truth, we do not need Christ or Christianity. To put it yet in a different fashion, to answer one of Wesley's lifelong concerns, if we have not lost the image of God why do we need to be renewed in holiness or be restored in the image of God?

I think there is a common element between Wesley's time and ours. Neither his time nor ours are very welcoming to a book telling us we are sinners. We are very prideful, think of ourselves as good, and deserving of all we receive and more.

Wesley's answer to Taylor is found in his "The Doctrine of Original Sin According to Scripture, Reason, and Experience." This document is the longest single piece Wesley writes during his long and fruitful career. In volume 9 of his "Works," it runs from page 192 to 464. It is written in several parts which were completed days apart as he turns from one area of his response to another. The dates are: November 30, 1756, January 18, 1757, January 21, 1757, March 23, 1757, March 24, 1757, and August 17, 1757. "A letter to John Taylor D.D." is written on July 3, 1759, which immediately follows his doctrine of original sin.

B. HISTORY AS PROOF OF ORIGINAL SIN

Wesley begins his defense of the doctrine of original sin in a very unusual but very interesting manner. He shows how sin has been evident in the whole history of mankind. This is a huge undertaking and in his presentation of this area he covers the wide sweep of history.

We modern Christians, at last Methodists, generally do not like to hear about our sins; much less do we like to confess them, even in our worship. Sometimes I think we are unaware of the complex, deep rooted, multileveled, and all pervading sin which is within and around us. In a sense we have become so familiar with sin we have accepted it as normal. We have in fact given other names to describe such acts and often these names tend to hide the real nature of sin. To say one is greedy, malicious, goes up the ladder at work without too many thoughts about others, bends the rules, makes it all sound so much better than to call these actions sin, but in many cases it's just what they are—sin. At the very least there is a component of sin in them.

He anticipated the psychological and sociological evidences of sin in a way which is remarkable for one writing in his time. Freud is not the first person to be aware that sin can be socially transmitted from one person to another as well as transmitted from one generation to another, as in father to son or daughter. The early Church Fathers as well as Wesley himself are aware of the sinful influences of the parents upon their children. The scriptures also bear witness to this fact.

Wesley's quadrilateral theological method is more on display in this work than in any of his others. He begins his defense of the doctrine of original sin by using the historical method. From there he moves to experience and finally on to the scriptures and the early Church Fathers.

Wesley's quadrilateral theological method is a way of understanding Christianity and what tools or methods we are to use to understand the Christian life. These tools keep us from going too far astray in our thinking and the actions we take as Christians.

The first tool we are to use is Christian tradition. By this Wesley means primarily the first century Fathers and the rich tradition of the Anglican Church. We Methodists today really have a much expanded view of tradition and therefore we consider the consensus of the faithful which not only includes the Early Fathers and the Anglican Church but the whole church from Biblical times until now. Methodists are open to learning from the tradition of the Roman Catholics, Lutherans, and Presbyterians, etc . . . We should do well, however, to once more study carefully the early Church Fathers because we have lost much of their teachings by being too caught up in our day, its experiences, and the current pop psychology. Where scripture is silent we can listen to tradition, especially the tradition of the early church for guidance.

The second is the Bible or Scriptures. One who reads much of Wesley will find himself constantly reading quotes from scripture. No other book by any author I have read quotes as much scripture in their sermons and tracts. His work is rich with passages from them. Wesley says he was a man of one book and this book is the scripture. He read extensively but the scripture was the final authority for his preaching and his thought. Scripture is often found in his writings as Wesley's thought and not so much as quotations found apart from his thoughts.

The third is reason. Reason is important because God has given it to man and if you exclude reason you cannot interpret the scriptures, Christian tradition, or experience. Reason has its limits but it is important and should be in the arsenal of the Christian. It is also true and important for us to remember Wesley said religion is a matter of the heart and not a matter of correct beliefs. This thought needs to temper our use of reason.

The fourth is experience and by experience Wesley means our experience with God and man. The experience Wesley is interested in is the experience which comes from reading the scriptures. To Wesley it is important to have his and others experience what he reads and understands from the scriptures. The Christian experiences which we have should be found in the scriptures. If the type of experience we are discussing as Christian and it is not found there one should be a little leery of calling such an experience Christian.

There are cases in which his experience and others went beyond, but were definitely not contradictory, to the scriptures. Two examples would be the doctrines of assurance and entire sanctification. He found these doctrines in the scriptures but he developed his teachings beyond what he finds there. If these doctrines were left undeveloped we would certainly be the loosers.

This is not meant to be an exhaustive study of the quadrilateral, merely a sketch to show Wesley uses these four tools to develop his theology. Some minor modifications must be made for us to use them today but they are remarkably few and they do not change our use of them in any significant way.

I want to know one thing,—the way to heaven; how to land safe on that happy shore. God himself has condescended to teach the way: For this very end he came from heaven. He hath written it down in a book. O give me that book! I have it; Here is knowledge enough for me. Let me be *homo unis libri.* Here then I am, far from the busy ways of men. I sit down alone: Only God is here. In his presence I open, I read his book; for this end, to find the way to heaven. Is there a doubt concerning the meaning of what I read? Does anything appear dark or intricate? I lift up my heart to the Father of Lights:—"Lord, is it not thy word, 'If any man lack wisdom, let him ask of God?' Thou 'givest liberally, and upbraidest not.' Thou hast said, 'If any be willing to do thy will, he shall know.' I am willing to do, let me know, thy will." I then search after and consider parallel passages of Scripture, "comparing spiritual things with spiritual." I meditate thereon with all the attention and earnestness of which my mind is capable. If any doubt still remains, I consult those who are experienced in the things of God; and then the writings whereby, being dead, they yet speak. And what I thus learn, that I teach.[3]

He believes we must go back to the beginning in order to really see how sin has so effectively infected all of us. One must remember when Wesley was writing and the knowledge and beliefs available to him at that time in order to fully understand the gigantic and remarkable sweep of his mind and his writings on original sin.

After the first sin and the consequent infection in man everything which has happened since has been affected by this infection. The abilities we have which can be used for good have become twisted and distorted. The heart has become deceitful. There is good in creation, we see it every day. In man, however, the good has forever been twisted and infected by sin. The scriptures again and again portray a story of man's sin.

Reading this area of Wesley's defense does not make us feel happy or uplifted. We are rather made to feel as if all is bad and all is evil. There is no escaping the study of history without finding the evidences of sin being ever present. Seldom if ever do we look at history from this perspective. In our historical studies we are usually thinking about dates and what happened at a certain time.

The story of Noah becomes a way for the theologian and Christian to see the corruption or infection of sin in history. It also shows the freedom which God gave to man becoming a way for man to express his opposition to God rather than his accepting God's love and agreeing to follow him. First there was Adam and Eve and they fell. They were expelled from the garden and mankind remained fallen and rebelled against God. Man continued in his sin and then God tried a flood and attempted to start over again with a few selected humans.

> Now, whatever particulars in this account may be variously interpreted, thus much is clear and undeniable,—that all these, that is, all the inhabitants of the earth, had again "corrupted their way;" the universal wickedness being legible in the universal punishment.[4]

---

3   Wesley, *Works*, 5:3-4
4   Wesley, *Works*, 9:197

Unfortunately the infection of sin in humanity did not end with Noah and the eight persons who were in the ark. Man once more shows his infection. One might wonder why this is true since these humans were selected from among all those on earth as worthy of being saved. Thus mankind would be starting over again and surely better. However, this did not happen. Man again showed his sinfulness.

Then think of man's history since the flood. There is the tower of Babel and the disintegration of one language for man. Language has become so infected with sin we have great difficulty communicating in an effective way with each other. Think of the consequences of our inability to effectively communicate and how this problem has persisted through the ages. This is a remarkably perceptive look at language Wesley provides for us.

Abraham was another new beginning or start for man but sin was evident soon there also. Sin was in all mankind even among the Israelites. Even though they were blessed with God's laws and the promises God made to them, they too were sinful. The advantages of being selected by God to be a blessing to mankind could not keep them from sin.

Then the Israelites were led off in the Babylonian captivity and the idolatry which was practiced before was only reduced and sin made its comeback. Some in the captivity returned to God but upon their return as the faithful remnant, sin regained its hold upon their leaders as well as the people. Idolatry, the replacing of God by anything else, returned once more. Man is shown to be remarkably persistent and consistent in his sinfulness.

Wesley looks at other nations as well, particularly the Romans. He discusses Hannibal, Cato the Elder, Pompey, and Caesar. These are great historical figures we have heard about, but for Wesley's purposes all of them show evidences of sin in their lives and in their cultures. Again, this is not the usual way we look at this history.

Then he turns his attention to more modern times. He discusses the heathens which for him mean those who do not believe in Christianity. One must remember he does not use this term in a negative sense as so many do. He discusses ancient as well as modern heathens and those in America as well as the American Indians. It should be noted by this time Wesley had visited America and returned to England and he no longer believed in the noble savage as did many of his contemporaries because he had seen them and had firsthand experiences with them.

Then he looks at the Asian and European cultures. He finds the effects of sin there as well. Even Africa came into his view. As one unalterably opposed to slavery, he saw sin at work there also. We know Wesley was opposed to the slave trade and worked against it until his death.

After looking at the non-theistic cultures of the world he turns his attention to the theistic cultures. He thought the Islamic wars were sinful.

One might think Wesley would be a little easier or softer on the Christian world, especially the Protestants, when he finally turns his attention to them. However, if this is what one thinks, then one would be vastly mistaken. He finds sin within Christianity, Roman Catholicism, Deism, Protestant nations, Great Britain, and Ireland. Everywhere he looks man is sinful. Every place he explores he finds the sin of man rampant. It's not a very pretty picture of mankind which is presented, but it is a true picture of all mankind from the Christian perspective.

Wesley believes war to be one of the greatest sinful acts man releases upon other men. Some men who are leaders are liable to think they need more territory so they can become even more powerful and feared. Everyone in the nation then seems to be brought into the warfare whether they want to be included or not and which is begun by only the few for own their benefit. National or regional pride is advanced and reason gets lost in the war along with the many who are mistakenly led to believe in the necessity and the moral correctness of the war.

But there is a still greater and more undeniable proof that the very foundations of all things, civil and religious, are utterly out of course in the Christian as well as the heathen world. There is a still more horrid reproach to the Christian name, yea, to the name of man, to all reasons and humanity. There is war in the world! War between men! War between Christians! I mean, between those that bear the name of Christ, and profess to "walk as he also walked." Now, who can reconcile war, I will not say to religion, but to any degree of reason or common sense?[5]

Wesley tells us to examine ourselves, and in doing so he goes deep into the makeup of English society itself. He discusses the life of sailors, officers of the Excise and Customs, tradesmen, merchants, the legal profession, nobility and gentry, priests and ministers.[6]

On a more personal note, Wesley even discusses the family itself. He urges us to look at ourselves, then our spouse, our children, servants, journeymen, neighbors, and tradesmen

> Why is the earth so full of complicated distress? Because it is full of complicated wickedness. Why are not you happy? Other circumstances may concur, but the main reason is because you are not holy. It is impossible, in the nature of things, that wickedness can consist with happiness.[7]

The purpose in presenting all of this material is not to show any dated idea Wesley may have had about his or any other cultures or religions. Our purpose is only to show Wesley finds man's sin in all of them, regardless of their country, time, leaders, or culture.

As a final conclusion of this section of his study of Original Sin (pages 192-238) Wesley summarizes his findings for us. "Still, then, sin is the baleful source of affliction; and consequently, the flood of miseries which covers the face of the earth,—which overwhelms not only single persons, but whole families, towns, cities, kingdoms,—is a demonstrative proof of the overflowing of ungodliness in every nation under heaven."[8]

Wesley is best known for and really preaches more about salvation and holiness in the Christian life, which is a positive and uplifting discussion. Yet it is interesting that his single longest treatise is not written on a positive or upbeat topic. Rather his longest is on the doctrine of original sin which can put a dampening effect on almost any discussion.

---

[5]   Wesley, *Works*, 9:221
[6]   Wesley, *Works*, 9:230
[7]   Wesley, *Works*, 9:235
[8]   Wesley, *Works*, 9:238

This is a message many of his followers in their more liberal, as well as other garb, have forgotten, or at least downplayed. The result intended or not, is when the doctrine of sin is downplayed, the remainder of the doctrines which Wesley preached are truncated and reduced in equal measure and thereby they lose the strength and forcefulness they really should have.

Once more, if there is little separation between man and God then Jesus has only to help with this little separation and thus the work God performs through the Christ is reduced to a small work. Perhaps it may be thought of by some as the last small step which allows a bridge over the small gap which separates us.

Wesley cannot and will not let us go down this road. The result of doing so is so devastating for Christianity he cannot allow us to make this mistake.

C. THREE SERMONS

Before going into the remainder of Wesley's argument here about original sin, a lost can be learned from him in three sermons he preached which clarify his thinking about original sin. They will help us understand where Wesley is coming from before we begin the arduous task of going through the remainder of his long and detailed tract. The first of these three sermons is entitled "The Deceitfulness of the Human Heart."[9]

Humans seem to be forever thinking more highly of themselves in some ways than they are in reality. Optimism and reveling in man and his achievements has something to say for it. Man has after all been able to do many good and important things. When this excessive optimism enters the religious realm and promotes the belief that therefore man is naturally good, virtuous, and well behaved, we are entering upon dangerous theological territory.

It is very easy for us to become enamored with our thoughts about man's growth and his wondrous potential. We then create ourselves as little Jack Horner's who say "what a good boy am I." Some may even go so far as to blame God for creating the problem of sin. Blaming others or even part of ourselves which we obviously control becomes the fashion of the

---

9   Wesley, *Works*, 7:335-43

day. We have to blame others for our sins and shortcomings. "See what you made me do" we say when in reality no one else makes us do anything. It is rather we who act, we who decide to sin, and we who blame everyone and everything else but ourselves.

Some say it's due to lack of education. It's as if they said, "If I just knew better I would obviously do better." Others think the problem comes from the movement of the blood or other actions of my body over which humans do not have control. Or, how can you blame me for doing what is commonly done by others? Some really extend themselves and blame the Devil as is found in the classic recent statement "the devil made me do it." It obviously is not me; something outside my control forced me to do it.[10] Even though I did it, and I know I did it, I say to myself and others the action is really not me. But if it is not me who acts, then who in reality is it?

The first two points of this sermon are: "The heart of man is desperately wicked," and the heart of man is "deceitful above all things.[11]

> See self-will, the first-born of Satan! "I will be like the Most High." See pride, the twin sister of self-will. Here was the true origin of evil. Hence came the inexhaustible flood of evils upon the lower world. When Satan had once transfused his own self-will and pride into the parents of mankind, together with a new species of sin,—love of the world, the loving the creature above the Creator,—all manner of wickedness soon rushed in; all ungodliness and unrighteousness; shooting out into crimes of every kind; soon covering the whole face of the earth with all manner of abominations.[12]

Pride and self-will are in man and these two are the origin of evil. We give attention and love these gods so much we replace the creator with our own creation. It is from self-will and pride all individual sins arise. We wind up either raising ourselves to the level of the creator and God or we glorify something which is not God and worship it. No matter how the sins work out, uniquely or the same, they all have this identical basis. Self-

---

10   Wesley, *Works*, 7:336
11   Wesley, *Works*, 7:337
12   Wesley, *Works*, 7:337

will and pride set loose in the world are infecting all humans. This is not something we have just learned, it has been with man for all the time we have known him as Wesley so brilliantly showed in his opening discussion of original sin.

> Hence, springs every species of vice and wickedness; hence every sin against God, our neighbor, and ourselves. Against God,—forgetfulness and contempt of God, of his name, his day, his word, his ordinances; Atheism on the one hand, and idolatry on the other; in particular, love of the world, the desire of the flesh, the desire of the eyes, and the pride of life; the love of money, the love of power, the love of ease, the love of the "honour that cometh of men," the love of the creature more than the Creator, the being lovers of pleasure more than lovers of God:—Against our neighbour,—ingratitude, revenge, hatred, envy, malice, uncharitableness.[13]

The heart is deceitful above all things. Self-will and pride lead to idolatry which leads us to think we are wiser and better human beings than the reality of them allows. We wind up deceiving ourselves as well as others. Rather than reading scripture, and thus finding our true condition, we rely on the dual roots of sin which are self-will, pride, and from them, idolatry. Because our hearts are full of deceit it is almost impossible for us to see ourselves as we really are. We are happy to deceive ourselves because the results appear to be in our favor.

The good news is there is hope for man even in his critical condition. The hope for man is for him to be born of God. Those who are so born are no longer desperately wicked. Indeed, they have been redeemed in righteousness.

> Only let it be remembered, that the heart, even of a believer, is not wholly purified when he is justified. Sin is then overcome, but it is not rooted out; it is conquered, but not destroyed. Experience shows him, First, that the roots of sin, self-will, pride, and idolatry, remain still in his heart. But as long as he continues to watch and pray, none of them can prevail against him. Experience teaches him, Secondly that sin (generally

---

[13] Wesley, *Works*, 7:340

pride or self-will) cleaves to his best actions: So that, even with regard to these, he finds an absolute necessity for the blood of atonement.[14]

The root of sin remains in man even though the root cannot prevail over man. Wesley is here making a distinction between justification in which sin is overcome and man is forgiven but the root of sin remains, and sanctification in which even the root of sin is gone. Sanctification or Christian perfection will be discussed in a later chapter so we will not deeply venture into distinguishing the two terms at this time.

Man can be justified only by the gift of God's grace. Further gifts of God are required in order for man to be sanctified. He concludes:

> Is it not wisdom for him that is now standing, continually to cry to God, "Search me, O Lord, and prove me; try out my reins and my heart! Look well, if there be any way of wickedness in me, and lead me in the way everlasting?" Thou alone, O God, "knowest the hearts of all the children of men:" O show thou me what spirit I am of, and let me not deceive my own soul! Let me not "think of myself more highly than I ought to think." But let me always "think soberly, according as thou hast given me the measure of faith!"[15]

The second sermon we will discuss is entitled "On the Fall of Man."[16] In this sermon Wesley introduces pain as the result of man's sin. If it were not for sin man would not suffer pain. "Why is there pain in the world; seeing God is 'loving to every man, and his mercy is over all his works?' Because there is sin: Had there been no sin, there would have been no pain. But pain (supposing God to be just) is the necessary effect of sin."[17]

Things began to unravel in the Garden of Eden when Eve listened to the serpent and believed a lie. She did not believe God and instead put her belief in the serpent's lies. In this way, she was deceived and gave more credit to the lies of the devil than she gave to the word of God. This is how

---

[14] Wesley, *Works*, 7:341
[15] Wesley, *Works*, 7:343
[16] Wesley, *Works*, 6:215-24
[17] Wesley, *Works*, 6:215

unbelief entered the world (un belief in God's word) or not believing God's word, and from unbelief came sin.

Adam's sin was different from Eve's. Even though he likewise ate of the same fruit, Adam was not deceived by the serpent. Adam sinned with his eyes open (he knew what he was doing). He thus rebelled against his creator and this rebellion created pain because in so doing Adam lost his innocence and his happiness. The moral part of the image of God was lost the instant Adam rebelled.

> Adam, in whom all mankind were then contained, freely preferred evil to good. He chose to do his own will, rather than the will of his Creator. He "was not deceived," but knowingly and deliberately rebelled against his Father and his King. In that moment he lost the moral image of God, and in part, the natural: He commenced unholy, foolish, and unhappy. And "in Adam all died:" He entitled all his posterity to error, guilt, sorrow, fear, pain, diseases, and death.[18]

God did not despise his creation, the work of his hands, even though the creation had fallen. God continued to work, to bring man back into a proper relationship with him. This work is found in the Old Testament as God prepared the world for his Son. God continued the work of his love for the world so he gave his Son and in so doing God gave us the remedy for all our sins.

> And here is a remedy for all our disease, all the corruption of our nature. For God hath also, through the intercession of his Son, given us his Holy Spirit, to renew us both "in knowledge," in his natural image;—opening the eye of our understanding, and enlightening us with all such knowledge as is requisite to our pleasing God;—and also in his moral image, namely, "righteousness and true holiness."[19]

The third sermon we will look at is on "Original Sin."[20] In it he covers some of the same material found in his much longer tract. Wesley begins

---

[18] Wesley, *Works*, 6:223

[19] Wesley, *Works*, 6:223

[20] Wesley, *Works* 6:54-65

with a view of the history of mankind which is a shortened version of the history which we have discussed. However, the result is the same—all men are sinful. His text for this sermon is "And God saw that the wickedness of man was great in the earth and that every imagination of the thoughts of his heart was only evil continually."[21] He relates this text to the very different images people in his day have of the wonders of mankind. The dignity, virtue, happiness, and the power of man are great according to the thought of the day. However Wesley is quick to say that man is not without sin.

When we look at scripture we find a very different concept of man presented and not just the text for this sermon.

> The Scripture avers, that "by one man's disobedience all men were constituted sinners;" that "in Adam all died," spiritually died, lost the life and the image of God; that fallen, sinful Adam then "begat a son in his own likeness;"—nor was it possible he should beget him in any other; for "who can bring a clean thing out of an unclean?"—that consequently we, as well as other men, were by nature "dead in trespasses and sins," "without hope, without God in the world," and therefore "children of wrath;" that every man may say, "I was shapen in wickedness, and in sin did my mother conceive me;" that "there is no difference," in that "all have sinned and come short of the glory of God," of that glorious image of God wherein man was originally created. And hence, when "the Lord looked down from heaven upon the children of men, he saw they were all gone out of the way; they were altogether become abominable, there was none righteous, no, not one," none that truly sought after God: Just agreeable this, to what is declared by the Holy Ghost in the words above recited, "God saw," when he looked down from heaven before "that the wickedness of man was great in the earth;" so great, that "every imagination of the thoughts of his heart was only evil continually."[22]

Not only does he find pride in man he also finds self-will. They have become a form of idolatry and from this idolatry we all suffer. Self-will

---

21   Wesley, *Works*, 54
22   Wesley, *Works*, 6:55

leads us to do what we want and to think we know better than our creator about what we are to do. We now follow our desires and our wills often without regard to others or to God himself.

Wesley, in what is an interesting thought for me, thinks we humans are able to sin more than the devil when he accuses us of loving the world.[23] By this Wesley means we seek to love the creature rather than the creator. We follow our fleshly desires rather than spiritual ones. Several appetites tend to lead us all down the wrong paths.

We also desire and love the honors and accolades we may receive from others because of the deeds we have performed.

> But if this be really so, if it be impossible to believe, and consequently to please God, so long as we receive or seek honour one of another, and seek not the honour which cometh of God only; then in what a condition are all mankind! The Christians as well as Heathens! since they all seek honour one of another! since it is as natural for them so to do, themselves being the judges, as it is to see the light which strikes upon their eye, or to hear the sound which enters their ear; yea, since they account it a sign of a virtuous mind, to seek the praise of men, and of a vicious one, to be content with the honour that cometh of God only![24]

Wesley then summarizes his findings in his sermon. First he says Christianity is different from heathenism because the heathen may say some or many people are evil but Christianity says all have fallen short of the glory of God. In Christian thought we all have been conceived in sin and are at enmity with God.

Second, if we deny this we are still heathens ourselves. Wesley says "that all who deny this, call it original sin, or by any other title, are but Heathens still, in the fundamental point which differences Heathenism from Christianity."[25] I again remind when Wesley uses the term "heathen" he is not using it in the sense of a bad person. He uses it as a term for one who is not a Christian.

---

[23] Wesley, *Works*, 6:60
[24] Wesley, *Works*, 6:62
[25] Wesley, *Works*, 6:63

Third, the proper nature of religion, or at least Christianity, is to heal the diseased soul. Our atheism is healed by the work God performs through Jesus and by God giving us the faith and conviction of God, that Christ loved me, died for me, and gave himself for me.

If man today was not a fallen creature he would need none of this, he would already be whole. The scriptures do not teach us we are whole, however. Just the reverse is true; we are in desperate need of a Physician.

> God heals all our Atheism by the knowledge of Himself, and of Jesus Christ whom he hath sent by giving us faith, a divine evidence and conviction of God, and of the things of God,—in particular, of this important truth, "Christ loved *me*, and gave himself for *me*."[26]

These three sermons give us John Wesley while he was not particularly responding directly to John Taylor and his book. These sermons do not differ in any way with his presentation of the doctrine of original sin but they do give us a perspective in understanding Wesley's complete and much longer version. They are in a sense much easier reading than the remainder of his Doctrine of original sin to which we now turn.

D. SCRIPTURE AND THE DOCTRINE OF ORIGINAL SIN

When we move to the next area of Wesley's tract on the doctrine of original sin, we have now moved to the much more difficult area for us to interpret and keep track of the discussion. From now on there are quotation marks galore and one has to be very careful in order to separate Wesley's comments from John Taylor's and others whom Wesley is quoting.

By this time in his writing Wesley has found a few others who have written about Original Sin in a way he can use. Now we must be careful to see who Wesley is quoting, be it John Taylor, David Jennings' "Vindication of the Scripture-Doctrine of Original sin," John Hervey's dialogue "Theron and Aspasio," Isaac Watts' "The Ruin and Recovery of Mankind," Samuel Hebden's "The Doctrine of Original Sin, as laid down in the Assembly's

---

[26] Wesley, *Works* 6:64

Catechism, explained," or Thomas Bolton's "Human Nature in its Fourfold State." Hervey was a member of the holy club at Oxford. Hervey and Wesley were close on this theological problem but they had their differences in other areas of Christian thought.

Because of the close reasoning and the method used by scholars to respond to another's work which was used in the time of Wesley, as well as the exegetical work being performed by Taylor and Wesley, it can be a challenge at times to separate who is being quoted and what Wesley is saying about it.

Before beginning his defense of the Scriptural Doctrine of original sin Wesley makes one short detour. He tackles the concept proposed by some that the reason more men are on the side of vice than virtue is due to poor education. The basis of this proposition is the concept of lack of good education. The thesis is if we just had more and better education more men would be on the side of virtue. What mankind needs they say is just to improve our educational system and mankind will be all right. This is the contention but Wesley does not accept the thesis that education, even good education, can replace true religion.

He destroys this argument by first agreeing that education is a fine thing and it does even better for us than we might imagine. However, how are we to account for this universal bad education which would be required in order to account for man's sin and also where did the good education come from out of the universal bad education in order to explain the presence of good men?

Take the example of the first parents. They were both wise and virtuous themselves or they weren't. If the first parents were not virtuous themselves, then the vice of their children did not come from proper education because it couldn't. Likewise, if the parents were virtuous and they taught their children to be virtuous how can one then account for the mess mankind is in now? So how does proper education change anything?

When we talk about original sin we are talking about the first sin. The first sin becomes a pattern or original for all the other sins which follow. Humanity was given freedom but we found a way to corrupt and adulterate our freedom. This is what humans have been doing since the origins of history.

The history of man is a history of fallen man and man corrupted by the infection of sin in ways which change all further communication. Men have all kinds of trouble understanding each other. The Biblical way of explaining and portraying this truth is to tell the story of Adam and Eve. In the Biblical account they fell from holiness, joy, communion with God, and happiness in a way which has decisively infected and impacted all the future history of man's freedom.

Each of us have become involved in the story of Adam and Eve because in reality, it is not just Adam and Eve's story it is the human story, it is the story of us all. What they did affects those who follow them just as what we do affects those who follow us. The consequences of Adam and Eve's sin affect others who follow just like the consequences of my sin affect those who follow me.

The evil we find in human history cannot be limited to following a bad example or a lack of proper education. This is not an adequate or complete explanation, though one might wish it to be true. Evil is much deeper than this and can adequately be explained only by the scriptural description of the sin which affects us all.

Scriptural history is nothing for man to brag about. When we read the Scriptures from the Old Testament until the coming of Christ we find sin in man. It is a history of the sin of faithlessness of man and the faithfulness of God. Even when Christ came all men were guilty.

> They teach us, that "in Adam all die:" . . . that "by" the first "man came" both natural and spiritual "death;" that "by" this "one man sin entered into the world, and in consequence of sin; and that from him "death passed upon all men, in that all have sinned."[27]

The discussion then turns to what punishment was given to Adam and Eve as a result of their sin. Taylor states the entire result of their sin to be only the death of the physical life and dismisses the spiritual life as being involved at all. According to this reasoning man is not really separated from God in the most important area of man's spiritual life. This definition and description of sin's punishment naturally is not to Wesley's liking.

---

[27] Wesley, *Works*, 9:240

Taylor says no other life is mentioned but Wesley points to the image of God which was mentioned earlier in the scripture, so he says the spiritual life is also in play.

Wesley quotes Hervey to make his point.

> "Adam violated the precept, and, as the nervous original expresses it, 'died the death.' He before possessed a life incomparably more excellent than that which the beasts enjoy. He possessed a divine life, consisting, according to the Apostle, 'in knowledge, in righteousness, and true holiness.' This, which was the distinguishing glory of his nature, in the day that he ate the forbidden fruit was extinct.[28]

The discussion then turns to the children of Adam and Eve and their descendents and whether or not they are or should be punished for Adam's sin. Taylor says Adam's posterity cannot be justly punished for what is Adam's exclusive sin. In this way Taylor diminishes the original sin and especially the results of original sin for mankind. Wesley commented:

> If no other was justly punishable, then no other was punished for that transgression. But all were punished for that transgression, namely, with death. Therefore, all men were justly punishable for it.
>
> By punishment I mean suffering consequent upon sin, or pain inflicted because of sin preceding. Now, it is plain, all mankind suffer death; and that this suffering is consequent upon Adam's sin. Yea, and that this pain is inflicted on *all men* because of his sin. When, therefore you say, "Death does descend to us in consequence of his transgression," . . . you allow the point we contend for; and are very welcome to add, "Yet it is not a punishment for his sin." You allow the thing. Call it by what name you please. "[29]

Jennings also supplies Wesley with some comments and clarification on this important matter.[30] Wesley finds "the death expressed in the original

---

[28]   Wesley, *Works*, 9:242
[29]   Wesley, *Works*, 9:242-3
[30]   Wesley, *Works*, 9:243

threatening, and implied in the sentence pronounced upon man, includes all evils which could befall his soul and body; death temporal, spiritual, and eternal."[31]

Taylor then uses the relation of Adam and Christ to say Christ raises from the dead all those who die because of Adam. This appears to be a universal rising of all men and Wesley says the scriptural passage used by Taylor (I Corinthians 15:21-22) is not given a true rendition by him. The scripture discusses the fact that those who die *in Christ* are raised from the dead, not all mankind, only those who are in Christ. Taylor says as in Adam all died, in Christ all are "undied" (do not die) or in other words, the death we die in Adam is the same death Christ "undies" in his work. In this discussion Taylor limits the death and undeath to the physical body. Wesley finds far more meant here than that. Physical and spiritual deaths are both involved in the work of Adam and Christ according to Wesley.

Following his argument Taylor talks about justification as something which comes upon all men because God's "abounding grace" has nothing to do with the consequences of Adam's sin. Wesley cannot remain silent in the face of such a terrible misunderstanding of the gospel.

> . . . what St. Paul says of abounding grace is simply this: (1.) The condemnation came by "one offence" only; the acquittal is from "many offences." (2.) They who receive this shall enjoy a far higher blessing by Christ than they lost by Adam. In both these respects, the consequences of Christ's death abound over the consequences of Adam's sin. And this whole blessing by Christ is termed, in the 18th verse, "justification;" in the 19th, "being made righteous."[32]

Wesley believes all mankind is sick and infected with sin as we have seen in his history of sin. This is the correct understanding of the status or condition of man. The scriptures best describe this condition by saying we all sinned in Adam. In some way we become sinners from the first defiant act by Adam and Eve. First there is the infection of sin and then the actual sin which naturally follows.

---

[31] Wesley, *Works* 9;245
[32] Wesley, *Works*, 9:253-4

This concludes the first part of Wesley's defense of the scriptural account of sin. Wesley gives us a good summary of the argument which has taken place thus far.

> It remains then, all that has been advanced to the contrary notwithstanding, that the only true and rational way of accounting for the general wickedness of mankind, in all ages and nations, is pointed out in those words: "In Adam all die." In and through their first parent, all his posterity died in a spiritual sense; and they remain wholly "dead in trespasses and sins," till the second Adam makes them alive. By this "one man sin entered into the world, and passed upon all men:" And through the infection which they derive from him, all men are and ever were, by nature, entirely "alienated from the life of God; without hope, without God in the world."[33]

E. THE ASSEMBLY OF DIVINES IN THEIR LARGER CATECHISM

The next phase of the argument turns to the Westminster Catechism, its scriptural basis, and how it is to be interpreted. Wesley says he has not subscribed to this particular catechism but he is willing to defend the points of the catechism with which he does not disagree.

Wesley determines, in agreement with Dr. Jennings, there are two types of texts in the Westminster Catechism. The first is a text directly proving the doctrine of original sin and the other is a text which illustrates the doctrine.[34] Taylor's main arguments against these propositions are they make it very difficult to have a creator God who is good and yet have so much evil and vice in the world. He also has a problem because the propositions of the catechism seem to reduce the freedom of man and man's moral accountability.

Wesley is able to counter these arguments very handily as we shall see. For now it is enough to say his doctrine of prevenient grace, which is God's grace given to every man, and which allows man to accept God's grace, plays a pivotal role. On the other hand, man can reject God's grace

---

[33]   Wesley, *Works*, 9:258
[34]   Wesley, *Works*, 9:261

because God's grace allows us this choice. In this manner, since God has given man the ability to accept God's grace, it is man who is responsible for the outcome i.e., accepting or rejecting God's prevenient grace. God would have us become his and fellowship with him, but we will not have it. In this way sin is man's responsibility and not God's because God has freely given us the way and the power for us to return to fellowship with him.

Rather than reducing man's freedom Wesley has not only increased it but he has likewise made us responsible for accepting God's grace or turning our backs on it. In this way he has made man a co-worker with God for man's salvation. As long as man accepts God's grace and grows in the Christian life he is working with God. God gives, but man has to accept, so man is responsible.

The first proposition is "The covenant being made with Adam as a public person, not for himself only, but for his posterity, all mankind descending from him by ordinary generation, sinned with him, and fell with him, in that first transgression."[35]

The best answer as to why sin is so universal is found in the Christian doctrine of original sin. No other answer, none, can adequately provide us with the reasons for universal sin. We can look for answers in education or its lack, psychology, or sociology all we want to but we will find there is no other adequate and so complete an answer to sin than the doctrine of original sin.

Adam is not just an individual but he is also a public person or the first person. As a public person Adam stands in for all of us. He is the first human created. The word of God to Adam not to eat the fruit of the tree, his doing so, and the consequences of his act are addressed thus not only to Adam but to all of mankind. In a sense then, we are Adam.

> This Scripture, therefore, is very pertinently quoted to prove what it is brought for. That 'Adam was a public person, including all his posterity, and, consequently, that all mankind, descending from him by ordinary generation, sinned in him, and fell with him in his first transgression,' . . .

---

[35] Wesley, *Works*, 9:262

The Scriptures pointed to in this argument center around Genesis 2:16-17 and Romans 5:12-20. Wesley declares the Winchester Proposition #1 as having been successfully defended and the argument won by the proposition.

The second proposition is "The Fall brought mankind into a state of sin and misery."[36] Taylor argues the only consequence of Adam's sin is he is now faced with physical death and so are all men who come after him.

Wesley counters with his argument that the scriptures say more is involved than just man's physical death. In addition, to his physical death, man's spiritual death and guilt are involved. In some manner all of mankind has become infected by sin. Consequently we now are all in a state of sin and therefore subject to the wrath of God.

The fall brought with it the loss of the image of God which Adam as our public person was first given and then in his act of rebellion lost for all of us. Shattered, twisted, distorted, is the image which is left and the spiritual part of the image of God was totally lost.

Taylor tries to say the death which came upon Adam and therefore all of us was a blessing and not a punishment for our sin. He tries to argue this by saying we receive more of God's graces as a result of the fall than we had before the fall. Wesley says the scriptures consider our physical death as a punishment and therefore Taylor's argument is false.

Wesley then summarizes:

> Be this as it may, it is certain, (1.) That mankind are now in a state of sin and suffering. (2.) That they have been so in all ages, nearly from the time that Adam fell. Now, if his fall did not bring them into that state, I would be glad to know what did.[37]

The third proposition is "Sin is any want of conformity to, or transgression of, the law of God, given as a rule to the reasonable creature."[38]

---

[36] Wesley, *Works*, 9:262
[37] Wesley, *Works*, 9:264
[38] Wesley, *Works*, 9:264

Wesley's argument is sin has infected all of us as a result of the fall and has become a part of the human condition. According to the scriptures we are sinful beings, and as such we are in a state or condition of sin.

The fourth proposition is "The sinfulness of that state into which man fell consists in the guilt of Adam's first sin; the want of that righteousness wherein he was created; and the corruption of his nature, whereby he is utterly indisposed, disabled, and made opposite to all that is spiritually good, and wholly inclined to evil, and that continually; which is commonly called original sin, and from which do proceed all actual transgressions."[39]

There is no way we can, by pretty words or fast shuffling of exegetical feet, avoid the scriptural account of our condition; we have come under the Divine wrath. When Adam fell and therefore mankind with him, he lost the righteousness with which he was created, and his nature was corrupted and wholly inclined to evil. This is called original sin and from this sin comes all other sins.

This proposition is a long one with many parts. Indeed it appears to almost be a summary of the entire doctrine of original sin itself. It covers the state of man after Adam's sin, his loss of righteousness, and the total corruption of his nature which is called original sin and from which all actual sins flow. Wesley takes each of these statements as a "proof" and comments on each of them after quoting Taylor.

Taylor argues the scriptures used by the Catechism do not say there are no exceptions to our unity with Adam. Wesley answers those scriptures which were quoted show when St. Paul was writing he meant everyone (Jew or Gentile) was in sin except for those who were "saved by grace."

Wesley then says "And who can find out a more rational way of accounting for this universal wickedness, than by a universal corruption of our nature, derived from our first parent?"[40]

The summary of this proposition for Wesley is the texts in the catechism which prove man's nature since the fall is deeply corrupted; we are inclined to evil and disinclined towards everything which is spiritually good. Therefore unless we receive God's grace we are unable to do anything which is pleasing to Him. But by the grace of God our sins may be forgiven.

---

[39] Wesley, *Works*, 9:264
[40] Wesley, *Works*, 9:266

Therefore Wesley says our true condition is if we chose not to accept God's grace it is our action which creates our continued condition. "We *may* live: but we *will* die.[41]" "And this easily accounts for the wickedness and misery of mankind in all ages and nations; whereby experience and reason do so strongly confirm this scriptural doctrine of original sin."[42]

The fifth proposition is "Original sin is conveyed from our first parents to their posterity by natural generation, so as all which proceeds from them in that way are conceived and born in sin."[43] It is not the sexual act in itself which is portrayed as sinful in this discussion. It is because our parents are sinful and cannot therefore pass on sinlessness; we of necessity are born in sin. If we are not born in sin there would be no necessity for God's saving action in Christ.

Sometimes the sin of one person can have repercussions and consequences in the lives of others. This is a truth we all have seen. We are together as humanity so sometimes the consequences of sin are indeed visited upon others.

For Wesley, starting with Adam and Eve an infection or corruption moves from one generation to another, working its way through all of humankind. There is no skipping of generations as the infection moves ever onward through all of us. There is nobody who starts sin free, with a clean slate, as though they have somehow been separated from the sinfulness of their parents and all the sinful history which has gone on before them.

God creates us as he does the oak tree through the acorn, Taylor argues. Thus, if a person is created and is created infected, God must have put the sin or infection in the person he just created because where else could it come from? Wesley obviously cannot accept this explanation of the scriptures. Wesley responds by saying God does not create man like an acorn. The truth is, sinful man propagates other sinful men—all this is true. "Yet God produces, in the sense above mentioned the man, but not the sin."[44] Wesley will not allow God to be the creator or source of sin. Sin comes from man, not God.

---

[41]   Wesley, *Works*, 9:275
[42]   Wesley, *Works*, 9:273
[43]   Wesley, *Works*, 9:275
[44]   Wesley, *Works*, 9:282

The sixth proposition is "The fall brought upon mankind the loss of communion with God, his displeasure and curse; (Gen. iii. 8, 10, 24 ;) so as 'we are by nature children of wrath,' (Eph. ii. 2, 3,) bond-slaves to Satan, and justly liable to all punishments, (2 Tim. ii. 26,) in this world, and that which is to come. (Gen. ii. 17; Rom. vi. 23.)"[45]

We can thus say we are deserving of the wrath of God. We have not and cannot do anything to deter that wrath. God originally (in Adam and Eve) created man's nature as pure and sinless. However, we now are infected or corrupted due to Adam's free choice which he could make because God created Adam and thus, all of us, with freedom of choice, at least to the extent we can cooperate with God or we can choose not to cooperate with him.

The seventh proposition is since the fall all mankind has lost communion with God and we have suffered his displeasure and curse, which is another way of saying we deserve and have incurred God's wrath and justly incur any punishments in this world and the next which God chooses for us.

Taylor does not believe communion with God was lost by Adam's sin. The only thing Christ did was to repair what little we lost due to Adam's sin. This particular work of Christ, Taylor says, is we will be raised up in the last day. Again, Taylor asks how in the name of justice can God hold us responsible for Adam's sin or how can God punish one person for another person's sin?

In response, Wesley further states though we are conceived and born in sin and can be called the children of wrath we have a Savior provided to us by God. This single act is able to prove God's justice and as well as his mercy.

Even though God is present everywhere we still do not have the close communion with him which we enjoyed before Adam sinned. God may surround us with his love but we don't have the intimate communion with him which both he and we desire.

Taylor concludes this discussion of the catechism by saying he has shown the consequences of Adam's first sin to be labor, sorrow, and mortality.[46] With this estimate Wesley disagrees saying Taylor has proven

---

[45]   Wesley *Works*, 9:282
[46]   Wesley, *Works*, 9:286

no such thing and to the contrary Wesley's points in this proposition have been proven. He then quotes Hervey who is quoting Mr. Howe about God being absent in us.

> He that invites you to take a view of the soul of man gives you but such another prospect, and doth but say to you, 'Behold the desolation!' All things rude and waste. So that, should there be any pretense to the Divine presence, it might be said, 'If God be here, why is it thus?' The faded glory, the darkness, the disorder, the impurity, the decayed state in all respects of this temple, too plainly show, 'the Great Inhabitant is gone!'"[47]

F. Objections, Questions, Redemption, and Regeneration

Next Wesley covers many of the answers Taylor gives to some objections which have been raised by his thinking and presented in his book and the connection between the doctrine of original sin and the doctrines of redemption and regeneration.

The first objection is "Are we not in worse moral circumstances than Adam was before he fell?[48] Taylor has three responses. If we are talking about the state of religion and virtue he says we are corrupt but this corruption is not man's nature, rather it is an abuse of man's nature.

Wesley responds to this by pointing out this description does not do justice to the ever present infection of sin in the history of man. How come all men partake rather than just some? Why, if their nature was not corrupt don't we have half of humanity corrupt and half virtuous? If men were no more turned towards vice than they are towards virtue, the split should be about half and half or equal it would appear.

If on the other hand, Taylor says we are talking about the means for spiritual improvement; those gifts we receive through Christ are greater gifts than Adam had before he sinned. Wesley responds by saying this is true for Christians but only 1/5 of the world are Christians so how have the other 4/5 of the world had their situation improved?

---

[47]   Wesley, *Works*, 9:288
[48]   Wesley, *Works*, 9:288

If we additionally are talking about moral abilities Taylor says the scriptures don't compare us with Adam. Therefore we are unable to judge the difference except by what Adam did before he sinned, with mankind today. Wesley says we can judge. When God created Adam he was good, there was no defect in him at all. There are defects in all of us now which Wesley has shown throughout this war, or doctrinal dispute.

Taylor says the Church Fathers have falsely elevated Adam's nature because such doctrine cannot be found in the scriptures. Wesley responds:

> They suppose Adam to have been created holy and wise, like his Creator; and yet capable of falling from it. They suppose farther, that through temptations, of which we cannot possibly judge, he did fall from that state; and that hereby he brought pain, labour, and sorrow on himself and all his posterity; together with death, not only temporal, but spiritual, and (without the grace of God) eternal. And it must be confessed, that not only a few Divines, but the whole body of Christians in all ages, did suppose this, till after seventeen hundred years a sweet-tongued orator arose, not only more enlightened than silly Adam, but than any of his wise posterity, and declared that the whole supposition was folly, nonsense, inconsistency, and blasphemy! [49]

The second objection is "But do not the Scriptures say, Adam was created after God's own image? And do his posterity bear that image now?"[50] Taylor says God created man in the image of God and in Genesis 9:6 when talking to Noah God says man shall not kill another man because he is made in God's image and from this Taylor concludes the image of God was therefore in humans at least in the time of Noah. He believes from this we can conclude men are still made in the image of God.

Wesley responds to this proposition by saying Adam was created in the image of God and when he fell there was some of the image left in man. He summarizes:

---

[49] Wesley, *Works*, 9:291

[50] Wesley, *Works*, 9:291

(1.) That man was created in the image of God. (2.) That this image consisted, not only in his rational and immortal nature, and his dominion over the creatures, but also in knowledge, actual knowledge, both of God and of his works; in the right state of his intellectual powers, and in love, which is true holiness.[51]

Yes, some of the image is left in man as has been discussed but the most important part of the image of God, the relationship with God, or the moral image portion of the image of God is completely lost.

The third objection is "but do we not derive from Adam a moral taint and infection, whereby we have a natural propensity to sin?"[52] Taylor says we have natural appetites and passions and sometimes they may receive too much attention and in so doing they may become sinful. However, this does not mean to him we can conclude man has a sinful nature. Just because some people at some time overdo things does not mean all of us overdo them all of the time.

Wesley says all men have "a natural propensity to sin. Nevertheless, this propensity is not necessary, if by necessary you mean irresistible. We can resist and conquer it too, by the grace which is ever at our hand."[53] The sickness and infection of sin is truly in all of us as Wesley has shown but there is a way for us to overcome this condition and that is by accepting God's grace and working with God for our salvation.

The fourth objection is "But do not the vices of parents often infect their children?"[54] Wesley says this cannot be denied. This statement is so evident there is no need to discuss it any further.

The fifth objection is "How can we account for children's beginning so soon to sin, but by supposing they have a natural propensity to it?"[55] Taylor's comment is basically that no one knows how soon children may begin to sin. To try to determine this is an impossible task for us to pursue. Wesley says it begins when children show revenge, self-will, and wrong

---

51   Wesley, *Works* 9:293
52   Wesley, *Works*, 9:293
53   Wesley, *Works*, 9:294
54   Wesley, *Works*, 9:294
55   Wesley, *Works*, 9:294-5

tempers which is just as soon as their faculties, especially reason, begin to show at all. So he places sin in children very easily and early.

The sixth objection is "Might not Adam's posterity be said to sin in him, as Levi is said to 'pay tithes in Abraham?'"[56] They don't find much to discuss which is relevant here.

The seventh objection is "'But there is a law in our members which wars against the law of our minds, and brings us into captivity to the law of sin and death.' And does not this prove, that we come into the world with sinful propensities?"[57] Taylor's first response is if their natures come into the world with us then there is no sin because our natures come from God. Remember the acorn theory of Taylor's that we are created fine, because if not it was God's fault. Wesley says if our natures come into the world and sinful propensities were irresistible then there is no sin but if they are resistible and we can conquer them, then there is sin. If we have some control, if we are given or have the ability to overcome sin, then if there is sin in us it must be because of our choice and not God's.

Taylor says in this particular case the Apostle was speaking only of a Jew under the power of sin and also it was to a Jew before the law was given to them. Wesley says the Apostle was born under the law and remained there until he became a Christian. Also, all Gentiles who were convinced of sin were under the law in the sense spoken of here. The description of the scripture given is of any Jew or Gentile ". . . who saw and felt the wickedness both of their hearts and lives, and groaned to be delivered from it."[58]

Now Taylor adds some questions. The first is "Is not the doctrine of original sin necessary to account for the being of so much wickedness in the world?"[59] Taylor says Adam's nature was not sinful but he managed to sin therefore the doctrine of original sin is not needed to explain sin in the world and it also cannot explain Adam's sin. There is no need for a doctrine of original sin because man's nature is not sinful, even if he does sin.

If mankind was equally poised between sin and virtue and mankind could choose one as well as the other he might buy Taylor's argument

---

[56] Wesley, *Works*, 9:296
[57] Wesley, *Works*, 9:296
[58] Wesley, *Works*, 9:297
[59] Wesley, *Works*, 9:300

Wesley says. He cannot believe this explanation, however, due to the sinfulness which he finds everywhere and in all generations.

The second question Taylor asks and answers is "How, then, are we born into the world?"[60] Taylor answers we are born without knowledge. All our sensual appetites and passions we are born with are good. God has created us good because God would not create us bad or evil.

Our appetites and passions might originally have been good but as they truly exist in us now they are not good says Wesley. Men may have and use reason to create and do many things, however the heart of man leads him astray and we are sinful even if we have the power of reason. Reason itself can be and is corrupted by the corruption of man.

The third question is "How far is our present state the same with that of Adam in paradise?"[61] The answers to this question are not worthy of an answer.

Taylor next turns his attention upon the relationship of the doctrine of original sin to the doctrines of redemption and regeneration.

For Wesley regeneration is not something we do for ourselves or which automatically happens to us. Regeneration is not normal; it is the gift of God's grace. The new birth is not the whole of sanctification; it is but the start of sanctification. An example of this process would be the birth of a child which is obviously not the completion of an adult but merely the entrance of the person into the world as a child.

In Wesley's view we cannot understand the power we have in the godly life unless we truly understand the doctrine of original sin. We cannot truly believe in Christ unless we are convinced of our own sin. Unless we believe we are ill we will not seek the help of a physician. If we do not believe in our sinfulness or our helplessness we are not going to believe in Christ or see a need for Him.

The doctrine of original sin does not reduce; rather it enhances moral behavior because it produces the repentance which prepares us for the life of love and faith. This life brings forth its fruits. This doctrine, instead of turning us away from God, turns us to God so we can trust only in his

---

[60] Wesley, *Works*, 9:300
[61] Wesley, *Works*, 9:302

grace. The knowledge that God is willing to save us from all our sins puts man in the position of choosing for God or rejecting his loving grace.

> The doctrine, that we are by nature "dead in sin," and therefore "children of wrath," promotes repentance, a true knowledge of ourselves; and thereby leads to faith in Christ, to a true knowledge of Christ crucified. And faith worketh love; and, by love, all holiness both of heart and life. Consequently, this doctrine promotes (nay, and is absolutely, indispensably necessary to promote) the whole of that religion which the Son of God lived and died to establish.[62]

The new birth is given by God's grace whereby we put on the new man in which we are changed inwardly and have the image of God renewed within us.

G. CONCLUSION

We must return to the crux of theology which is the doctrine of original sin. The further away we stray from this firm foundation the more difficult the rest of our Christian doctrines are to understand and preach. Way too often today we try to preach or think without having the foundation of original sin to give us the reason and rationale for the rest of Christian doctrine and the Christian life. Christianity can quickly become a floating ethic founded upon the "love of God" about which we have lost the depth of meaning in our understanding. Because we don't really understand our condition we are in no position to ask for or receive the proper prescription for it.

Our daily papers expose us to man's sinfulness all over the world but we don't think of it in this way. We think of it as a "sound bite," as vignettes of what's going on in the world. We think it's too bad about this or that situation, those people starving, husbands and wives hurting and killing one another, rape, murder, incest etc . . .

It has been truthfully said the only Christian doctrine which can be supported by empirical evidence is the doctrine of original sin. It all starts here, this is the foundation.

---

[62]   Wesley, *Works*, 9:312

It is impossible to make laws which will keep people from sinning. We have tried it unsuccessfully and God gave us the law long ago and it has not stopped man from sinning. We can't resolve sin with better education, economics, or politics. It can be changed only by accepting God's grace and entering the new birth, which has been made possible for us by God's loving sacrifice which he made through his Son, our Lord, Jesus the Christ. And, this we do one person at a time.

If humanity is getting better and better day by day and that in every way as Taylor and others may argue, there is no explanation for the universality of sin. The best answer comes to us by exploring the terrible depths and breadths, the horrible separateness we feel from God by studying and believing in the Biblical concept of original sin. No other explanation is capable of explaining our condition so completely.

2

THE PREVENIENT GRACE OF GOD

A. INTRODUCTION

The second theological war Wesley has and which we will discuss is with predestination, or election, or double predestination. This is the concept that God has determined from before creation those who would be saved and those who would not be saved—they would be damned. This theological war was a complex war because many Christian ideas or concepts are at stake.

The power and knowledge of God are a part of this war. If God is all powerful he can surely save those he wants to but if man is able to stand up to God and say "no" doesn't this limit the power of God? Also, if God knows everything he surely knows those who will be saved, so man has a very limited freedom because God has decided who will be saved and who won't.

The relationship between grace and the free will of man is a part of this war. Is God's grace given only to the few he has already decided shall receive it or is God's grace for all and if for all how does this relate to God's power and how does all this relate to the freedom of man's will or does man have any free will in regard to man's salvation?

Several good questions are asked, debated, and answered in this theological war of Wesley's which discusses many issues of interest to us.

We today have rarely heard many sermons of the true double predestination variety, perhaps except for a few staunch believers. In

Wesley's day the issue was hotly debated with few prisoners taken and certainly no timeouts were asked for or given.

This war was particularly difficult for Wesley because many members of his societies and other followers were believers in predestination and among his clergy two very well known were among them. George Whitefield, a member of the holy club and friend of Wesley's during the Oxford days, was one and another was Augustus Toplady.

Also Lady Huntingdon who was an associate of the Wesley's for years fell under the sway of the doctrine of predestination. She founded a college which supported that doctrine. She was very concerned about some of the thinking of the Wesley's and eventually fired an able person from the college because he followed the Wesley's thought rather than hers. The cousin of Lady Huntingdon, Walter Shirley, weighed in with a circular letter saying the Wesley's thought as expounded in the 1770 Conference Minutes was dreadful heresy.

Dueling conferences were proposed by Shirley and others in their efforts to put the predestination view forward. They were not successful in this attempt.

Rowland Hill, one of Countess of Huntingdon's preachers, wrote against John Fletcher, who in turn, was writing for John Wesley. Then Rowland's brother, Richard, also wrote against Fletcher.

Wesley answered Richard by showing some of his logical inconsistencies and many of his other errors.

Though normally close to Calvin in most doctrines, this was one doctrine Wesley could not agree to. In fact he found it not only untrue in some renditions of it but also a very misleading doctrine in others. In some respects, and at different times, he tried to write as close to Calvin and election as he could but in others he let go and pushed the differences to the maximum.

It is difficult to explain any theological concept without placing it with others which are dynamically related to it and consider how each influences the others. This is particularly true of Wesley because much of his theology concerns the order of salvation and to understand his concepts we need to consider those doctrines which go before and often those which follow in order to set the particular doctrine we are studying in its place. Only in this way is one able to fully grasp his thought. We will follow this advice as we consider the doctrine of prevenient grace.

Thus, in order to fully understand Wesley's doctrine of prevenient grace we must see how that doctrine relates to and fits with the doctrines of sin, original sin, election and reprobation, and natural man, because they are all bound up with each other.

B. ADAM'S (AND EVE'S) FALL

Probably most modern scholars would regard the Garden of Eden as a myth or story, though not in the sense of its being a lie or something which is untrue. These narratives would be considered as stories with great depth and symbolic meaning which are able to speak volumes about the relationship of God with man both as it should be and as it really is.

In the Biblical story of the fall we find such themes covered as what man was created to be and what he has instead become. The sin in man is wonderfully presented. The Biblical story declares man is a sinner, one who sins against God, putting himself in the place of God, and following his own desires rather than the will of God. We likewise find an explanation for pain in childbirth, why man has to work to survive, and even our animosity to snakes. It covers our relationships with the rest of God's creation as well as any number of additional things.

Wesley approaches the Garden of Eden and Adam and Eve narratives a bit differently. Though he is aware of and discusses these themes and more, he believes the Garden of Eden narratives to be historical reality. In this reality we were created to live our lives with God and enjoy this wonderful relationship forever.

The act of disobedience by Adam and Eve and the consequences of this act are not limited to them. The consequences of this act have been visited upon all mankind. No child of man escapes unscathed from this ancestral act. All the descendents of Adam participate in this sin, and even further, Adam has become the human father of us all. Thus, all the descendents of Adam participate in sin because of him. The result of this act of Adam and Eve is found in our lives. We are damaged goods, rotten, perverse, and no longer acceptable to God. Looked at from the point of view of the order of salvation, we have completely fallen from Him. No longer do we have the intimate relationship with God enjoyed by our parents, Adam and Eve, before their disobedience and rebellion against God. We have no way of restoring this relationship with God because we have broken it, denied it, and turned our backs on it by placing ourselves in the position of God.

The complete discussion of Wesley's views on original sin are found in Chapter 1 and do not need to be repeated here. It is enough to remember them as we proceed.

C. NATURAL MAN'S CONDITION BEFORE GOD

In Wesley's day there must have been a lot of discussion about natural man. We find many such allusions in his discussion of original sin and it certainly is a part of Wesley's discussion of predestination and prevenient grace.

Natural man did not come into being until after the Fall of Adam and Eve. Before the fall there was no such person because Adam and Eve were in that intimate, personal, loving relationship with God and there were no other human beings in existence. The image of God was complete in them.

Wesley handles the condition of natural man in one of his Standard Sermons, "The Spirit of Bondage and Adoption." [1]

The first thing Wesley says about natural man is he is asleep. None of the spirit and spiritual senses has been awakened and he therefore does not know spiritual good or evil. The eyes of his understanding are closed and because of this he cannot see spiritual realities. There are no openings through which knowledge of spiritual things may come. Natural man is therefore ignorant of what he should most be concerned to know. Obviously he is ignorant of God. The conclusion of this point is:

> He has no conception of that evangelical holiness, without which no man shall see the Lord; nor of the happiness which they only find whose 'life is hid with Christ in God!'[2]

---

[1]   Wesley, *Standard Sermons*, 1:178-98
[2]   Wesley, *Standard Sermons*, 1:182

Wesley reasons further, because this man is spiritually asleep, he is in a sense at rest. There is a kind of security such a man finds because he is unaware of spiritual things. Indeed, if one were blind and standing next to a hole or pit one would be oblivious to the danger lurking at the very next step. Such a person undoubtedly would not be trembling or concerned for the danger he is in because he would be totally unaware of the danger which is so close.

In religious terms we would say such a person is in no fear or dread of God or the consequences of his life because he is not aware of them and therefore cannot understand them. Because he is asleep and blind to spiritual realities he may even think the blameless life resides in the actions he performs rather than in the inner truths of religion. Or, in an unusual turn of events, he may think he has no obligations to God since Christ came to destroy the law and the prophets. Since Christ destroyed them he may believe he is consequently saved in his sin rather than from his sin. Therefore he believes that he can go to heaven without really understanding God's words or His Son.

> The characteristic feature of the natural condition in which sin has come to feel at home is a bondage that is unconscious of its plight, analogous to the state of moral sleep, or ethical unconsciousness—unawareness of any serious moral hazard.[3]

The third element of man's condition is he really does not understand himself and the spiritual realities of his life. Such a man may talk about repenting at some time in the future, at least some time before he dies. Unfortunately we do not know when the time of our death will come or under what circumstances it will be. It is therefore not certain we will have the leisure to repent when we decide it is time to make the effort.

For some reason Wesley finds the ignorance of natural man most strongly represented by those we would think of as men of learning. If such a natural man is indeed a man of learning he may talk about man's rational abilities, the freedom of man's will, and the necessity of such free will in order for men to be moral.

---

[3] Oden, *John Wesley's Scriptural Christianity*, 279-80

Further, the man who is asleep or blind may be able to have a kind of joy. He would be able to congratulate himself because of the wisdom and goodness he sees within himself. As long as he is able to do well for himself others may look at his life and speak favorably of him. Such observers may even say he is a happy man.

This man who is asleep or blind may likewise come to believe he has great liberty. He may even think he is free from the errors of the common man and the prejudices of the educated man. In all this it is certain he is free from the wisdom which comes only from God.

Christians know this blind or spiritually asleep man to really be a servant of sin. However, even though such a person is a servant of sin he is not troubled because in his sleep he feels no condemnation. He is able to say and believe man is weak and frail. If such a person ever has a true religious thought he can easily stifle it by reminding himself he should have no fear for himself because God is merciful and Christ died for sinners.

> Thus, he remains a willing servant of sin, content with the bondage of corruption; inwardly and outwardly unholy, and satisfied therewith; not only not conquering sin, but not striving to conquer, particularly that sin which doth so easily beset him.[4]

There is another way to look at this and this is how Wesley describes the condition of natural man. This second way is not contradictory to the first in any manner at all, it is just another way looking at or describing the same thing. It is as though Wesley is saying if you don't understand this description I'll give you another.

Wesley starts with the concept of God creating man in God's own image. This image of God is composed of three elements. The first part is the *natural image* which means we were created like God in our immortality and we were given freedom of the will. This is a very important part of the image of God in Wesley's view as we will see later. The second part is we were given the *political image* of God, which means man was given power and control over the earth. After all, man names the animals, fish, and birds and has power over them. The third part of the image of God is

---

4   Wesley, *Standard Sermons*, 1:185

an extremely important part which Wesley calls the *moral image* of God, which is righteousness and holiness.

Because of his rebellion against God and God's will, man then died to God and the moral image of God was destroyed in him. This death is not a physical death but a spiritual one and therefore it is more important and has greater consequences for man than would be a physical death alone.

> . . . He died to God,—the most dreadful of all deaths. He lost the life of God: He was separated from Him, in union with whom his spiritual life consisted. The body dies when it is separated from the soul; the soul, when it is separated from God . . . So he had lost both the knowledge and the love of God, without which the image of God could not subsist.[5]

Natural man may be twisted and distorted in the first two parts of God's image in us, the natural and political, but the moral image is gone. The point of contact between man and God is no more.

Natural man is spiritually dead and in peril of eternal death. He has no chance for salvation because he is separated from God who is the source of salvation. Man has supplanted God, and rebelled against Him as the ruler of his life. Without accepting God as his Lord, the remaining capacities and abilities of man from the image of God are now distorted and twisted.

Wesley gives an excellent summary of his thinking.

> *But the natural man*—That is, every man who hath not the Spirit; who has no other way of obtaining knowledge, but by his senses and natural understanding. *Receiveth not*—Does not understand or conceive. *The things of the Spirit*—The things revealed by the Spirit of God, whether relating to His nature of His kingdom. *For they are foolishness to him*—He is so far from understanding, that he utterly despises, them. *Neither can he know them*—As he has not the will, so neither has he the power. *Because they are spiritually discerned*—They can only be discerned by the aid of that Spirit, and by those spiritual senses, which he has not.[6]

---

5   Wesley, *Works*, 6:67
6   Wesley, *Notes*, 591

D. Natural Man's Reality

After taking all this time to discuss Wesley's view of natural man it may come as a shock to find out he did not believe in the existence of natural man at all, at least natural man as we have described and discussed him.

By definition natural man is man completely apart from God. The image of God in man has been broken, twisted and distorted; at least this is true of the natural and political portions of the image of God. The moral image has been completely destroyed and is gone as we have said. Not only is there no saving relationship, there is no relationship with God at all. That intimate, spiritual, life giving umbilical cord has been severed and therefore no life giving spirit of God comes through it to give man life and spiritual sustenance.

In his sermon "On Working Out Our Own Salvation" Wesley shows he does not believe in the existence of natural man. On this point some of the stronger commentators on Wesley's theology agree. Umphrey Lee, Colin Williams and Harald Lindstrom as well as many others all agree Wesley does not believe in the reality of natural man. However, after spending so much time describing and discussing natural man and what happened to man as a result of the sin of Adam and Eve, how can Wesley say natural man does not exist? What reason or reasons are given by him for this discussion at all? How can such a concept be important if it is just that, only a concept without any basis or person in reality for us to see? Let's see how Wesley gets out of this one.

E. Prevenient Grace

Wesley's theology comes very close to Calvin's at the point of man's sin and separation from God. For instance John Wesley would have no problem with Calvin's definition of sin.

> Sin makes a division between man and God, and turns the Divine countenance away from the sinner. Nor can it be otherwise; because it is incompatible with his righteousness to have any communion with sin. Hence the Apostle teaches, that

man is an enemy to God till he be reconciled to him through Christ.[7]

How far away is this from Wesley's definition?

> Q. 15. In what sense is Adam's sin imputed to all mankind?
> A. In Adam, all die; that is (1.) Our bodies then become mortal. (2.) Our souls died; that is, were disunited from God. And hence, (3.) We are all born with a sinful, devilish nature. By reason whereof, (4.) We are children of wrath, liable to death eternal. (Rom. V.18; Ephes.ii.3)[8]

The divergence between Wesley and Calvin concerns God's action towards man not man's condition apart from God. It is the doctrine of prevenient grace which gives Wesleyan thought some of its distinctiveness. Especially is this true because of how Wesley couples it with his doctrine of Original Sin. Prevenient grace is God's grace which is a work of God within the heart of every man. Calvin may find God's grace lacking for some people but Wesley believes there is no man who lives apart from this grace of God. Though all mankind receives this gift of God's grace, the difference between us lies in our response to this grace. Some receive this grace and turn away from God but others receive this grace, accept it, respond to it, and continue to receive more and more grace until they reach salvation.

Wesley discusses our natural conscience but he finds this natural conscience to be anything but natural. Our conscience is God's grace which Wesley calls preventing or prevenient grace.

> Every man has a greater or less measure of this, which waiteth not for the call of man. Every one has, sooner or later, good desires; although the generality of men stifle them before they can strike deep root, or produce any considerable fruit. Everyone has some measure of that light, some faint glimmering ray, which, sooner or later, more or less, enlightens every man that cometh into the world. And every one, unless he be one of the small number whose conscience is seared with a hot iron, feels more or less uneasy when he acts contrary to the light of his

---

7   Calvin, *A Compend of the Institutes of the Christian Religion*, 110
8   Wesley, *Works*, 8:277

own conscience. So that no man sins because he has not grace, but because he does not use the grace which he hath.[9]

Wesley locates the prevenient or preventing grace of God in our conscience, where the actions of our conscience become the supernatural workings of God in man's life.

Wesley believes even those of other religions, heathens, and any others, in fact all men have received this supernatural gift of God. This prevenient grace in the conscience is the light which God gives to every man.

Collins finds two definitions of prevenient grace in Wesley. The first he calls the narrow definition and by it means the grace of God's which is given to man before justifying and sanctifying grace. It also leads to a person's being convinced or convicted they are a sinner. The second or broader definition of prevenient grace is all of God's graces because God's grace comes to us before we are able to accept or reject that grace. All of God's graces thus come before man's acceptance or rejection of them and therefore it is prevenient. However Wesley usually uses the term in the narrow sense and we will be using it in the narrow sense throughout this discussion.[10]

All of God's works within man are by God's grace. There is no natural man as we have seen, but there is natural man plus God's prevenient grace; this is the true condition or description of man.

A modern interpreter of predestination, Wayne Grudem, in an otherwise strong and able presentation, presents a definition or description which seems confused, contradictory, and not convincing to me.

. . . we must affirm that the doctrine of election is fully able to accommodate the idea that we have a voluntary choice and we make willing decisions in accepting or rejecting Christ. Our choices are voluntary because they are what we want to do and what we decide to do. This does not mean that our choices are absolutely free, because . . . God can work sovereignly through our desires so that he guarantees that our choices come about as he has ordained but this can still be understood as a real choice because God has created us and he ordains that such a

---

9   Wesley, *Works,* 6:512
10   Collins, *The Scripture Way of Salvation,* 40

choice is real. In short, we can say that God causes us to choose Christ voluntarily.[11]

Wesley states the conscience has a threefold job to perform within us. The first is as a witness who tells us what we have done by our thoughts, words or actions. So we are made aware of what we have done which is for good or for ill. Without our conscience we would not be aware of our actions. The second action our consciences perform is as a judge whereby it passes judgment upon what we have done and said. It informs us if these actions have been good or evil. This judgment is from God's prevenient grace, informing us of the rightness or wrongness of our actions. Such informing may be very weak in our minds. The third function it performs in us is in some way to execute a judgment or sentence upon us. We receive some measure of complacency when what we have done through thought, word, or action is good and by the same token it gives us a degree of unease if our actions have not been good.

Wesley is adamant in saying there is absolutely nothing which man can do to deserve or earn his salvation. At this point man is utterly helpless and unable to do anything from his side to heal the separation from God which would bring us back together.

Since Wesley cannot allow man's knowledge of God to arise out of man he has to find a way of explaining how man can come by such knowledge. He is also unwilling to have this knowledge come as Calvin says, by irresistible means. This problem is wonderfully solved by the doctrine of prevenient grace. As Sugden, Wesley's editor of the Standard Sermons says:

> He (Wesley) avoided Pelagianism by his definite teaching that through the Fall man became totally depraved, dead in trespasses and sins, without any power to resist temptation or to turn to God; but he also avoided Calvinism by his doctrine of prevenient grace, to wit, that the Holy Spirit is given to every man to reveal to him his duty and to give him power to turn to God for help and salvation [parenthesis mine]. This free gift, he

---

[11]   Grudem, *Systematic Theology*, 680

taught, comes to ALL men unto justification of life; and this true light enlightens every man that cometh into the world.[12]

By his doctrine of prevenient grace Wesley avoided the two other ways of explaining the problem, both of which he thought were errors. The first error is Pelagianism. The doctrine of Pelagianism states there is no original sin and because of this man has within himself the power and ability to choose the right path and thereby remain sinless. Wesley could not believe this because he believed sin was real and his doctrines of sin and original sin would not fit with such an aberration of Christian thought.

The second error avoided is election and reprobation, the predestination doctrines of Calvinism. Predestination is the doctrine stating before the creation of the world God decided who would be saved (elected) and who would be denied salvation (reprobated).

> We shall never feel persuaded as we ought that our salvation flows from the free mercy of God as its fountain, until we are made acquainted with his eternal election, the grace of God being illustrated by the contrast—viz. that he does not adopt promiscuously to the hope of salvation, but gives to some what he denies to others. It is plain how greatly ignorance of this principle detracts from the glory of God, and impairs true humility.[13]

Or again,

> It is the election of God, which makes this difference between men. We are not afraid to allow, what Paul very strenuously asserts, that all, without exception, are depraved and addicted to wickedness; but with him we add, that the mercy of God does not permit all to remain in depravity. Therefore, since we all naturally labour under the same disease, they alone recover to whom the Lord has been pleased to apply his healing hand. The rest, whom he passes by in righteous judgment, putrefy in their corruption till they are entirely consumed . . . [14]

---

[12] Wesley, *Standard Sermons*, 2:43-44

[13] Calvin, *Institutes*, 3:21:1, 203

[14] Calvin, *A Compend of the Institutes of the Christian Religion*, 53

Because of his doctrine of prevenient grace Wesley is able to maintain the sinfulness of man. Man is separated from God and spiritually dead. He is also able to protect God's initiative in the process of salvation. God is the single source of everything in the order of salvation and to him belongs all the glory.

F. Man's Responsibility

So far we can see the consistency and the meaningfulness of how these doctrines of Wesley fit together. However there is still one last piece we need to add to the rest in order to get the full sweep of Wesley's theology.

The correct understanding of it is every grace comes from God, starting with his prevenient grace. It is good that we have managed to avoid the twin perils of Pelagianism and Predestination, of election and reprobation, but our presentation is not yet complete without the final link.

The final piece of this theological puzzle is man's response to the prevenient grace which God has given him. Williams says it so well: "Thus because God is directly at work even within the natural man, man is responsible; not because he is naturally free to do God's will, but because he resists God's grace. This is not to say this prevenient grace, apparent in the conscience, is enough to enable man to turn to God in faith. Further gifts of grace are necessary to enable man to come to repentance and then to justification."[15] We see God's prevenient grace is not irresistible; man can deny it, turn his back on it, and not claim it. It is however by God's grace we are given the ability and allowed to accept Him and his grace. Because of God's grace we have a choice,[16] and the point of our having that choice is made by Wesley quite often.

> . . . For he has made you free agents; having an inward power of self-determination, which is essential to your nature. And he deals with you as free agents from first to last. As such, you may shut your eyes as you please. You have sufficient light shining all around you; yet you need not see it unless you will. But be

---

[15]   Williams, *John Wesley's Theology Today*, 42

[16]   Lindstrom, *Wesley and Sanctification*, 37

assured, God is not well pleased with your shutting your eyes, and then saying, "I cannot see."[17]

Wesley even says the sin of Adam was allowed by God. He did not create Adam so Adam was unable to· sin; Adam was created with the freedom to choose good or evil, else why would he have told Adam and Eve about the tree of which they should not eat the fruit? God did not put the evil in man but allowed man to make the choice for evil. If man was incapable of sin because of God's irresistible grace there would have been no sin. Only if man was given the ability to choose could there be sin because the other alternative would be that God implanted evil within man and this Wesley will not allow.[18]

Perhaps no better description of this situation of man's choice can be given than is found in one of the Wesleyan hymns.

> Sinners, turn, why will ye die?
> God, your Maker, asks you why:
> God, who did your being give,
> Made you with himself to live;
> He the fatal cause demands,
> Asks the work of his own hands,
> Why, ye thankless creatures, why
> Will ye cross his love, and die?
>
> Sinners, turn, why will ye die"
> God, your Saviour, asks you why:
> God, who did your souls retrieve,
> Died himself, that ye might live.
> Will you let him die in vain?
> Crucify your Lord again?
> Why, ye ransom'd sinners, why
> Will you slight his grace, and die?
>
> Sinners, turn, why will ye die?
> God, the Spirit, asks you why:
> He who all your lives hath store,

---

17 Wesley, *Works*, 6:311
18 Wesley, *Notes*, 71

Woo'd you to embrace his love:
Will you not his grace receive?
Will you still refuse to live?
Why, ye long-sought sinners, why
Will you grieve your God, and die?

Dead already? Dead within,
Spiritually dead in sin:
Dead to God, while here you breathe,
Pant ye after second death?
Will you still in sin remain.
Greedy of eternal pain?
O ye dying sinners, why,
Why will you for ever die?[19]

Looked at in another way we must conclude God has given man the power or capacity to sin. God has given us the strength, the ability, and the intelligence to sin. He has equipped us so we can sin because without these abilities God has given us we would not be able to sin. But just because God has given us the ability and power to sin we cannot conclude God is the author of man's sin. Man is negligent in his stewardship of these powers given to him by God and chooses evil rather than good.

Wesley may not complete or present as strong a case for original sin as some would like and many think he could do a better job in discussing how a righteous man can have sons of iniquity, but they unite in saying he has given us many helpful concepts of the sin of man. After all, Wesley spent over 300 pages arguing as a systematic theologian about Original Sin.

The conclusion of this area can be summed up by saying there is no such thing as natural man, as man totally separated from the love of God because of God's prevenient grace. Only those who have denied this grace are totally separated from God and this separation is by their own choice, and even then Wesley is not sure he has ever met a man who is totally without the working of prevenient grace within his life.

> . . . the initiating operations of the Holy Spirit as manifested in prevenient (and other) grace removes "all imagination of merit

---

[19] Wesley, *Wesley's Hymns*, no.6, vv.1-4

> from man," while at the same time it increases human ability and, consequently, human responsibility as well . . . Simply put, the empowering grace of God is already present, even before we are fully aware of its presence. More important, perhaps, this grace ever invites response. The grace of God meets us at our present level and then beckons us to go further[20].

Thus man is responsible for the light which God has given to him. He has given us the power to choose him which he desires, but men are nonetheless able to deny him by choosing not to accept his grace.

We are to work out our own salvation by the grace of God. We are participants with God because he has first, by grace, allowed us to respond to him through prevenient grace.

> Therefore, inasmuch as God works in you, you are now able to work out your own salvation. Since he worketh in you of his own good pleasure, without any merit of yours, both to will and to do, it is possible for you to fulfill all righteousness. It is possible for you to "love God, because he hath first loved us;'" and to "walk in love," after the pattern of our great Master. We know, indeed, that word of his to be absolutely true: "without me ye can do nothing." But, on the other hand, we know, every believer can say, "I can do all things through Christ that strengtheneth me.[21]

G. PREVENIENT GRACE VS. PREDESTINATION (ELECTION AND REPROBATION)

Now we are going to take all we have learned about prevenient grace and see how it fits with the doctrine of Predestination. They obviously do not agree, but we will see how Wesley's doctrine of prevenient grace allows him to avoid predestination and in fact provide a strong answer and rebuttal to it.

---

[20] Collins, *The Scripture Way of Salvation*, 44-45
[21] Wesley, *Works*, 6:512

1. UNDERSTAND HOW SOME PEOPLE GET TO THIS POSITION

The longest single document of Wesley's concerning this topic is to be found in his "Predestination Calmly Considered"[22] of 1752, which in the "Works" are fifty-five pages long. Because of this we will spend some time discussing this important document. Wesley has put a good deal of thought into this presentation.

He begins his thought by telling those who disagree with him and who are predestinarians and/or reprobation believers he can readily understand how they came to such conclusion. After all there are many places and writings they could go to which would mislead them and apparently confirm their beliefs.

He also believes some Christians truly have had God deal with them at some time in a manner which seems to them to preclude them telling the Divinity "no." Since these Christians have had this particular experience it is not a far step for them to next believe God works in everybody this exact same way and perhaps even further, God works in everybody at all times in this way. In other words, the Christian may be led to conclude God always works irresistibly in every believer. Also, if God always works this way with the believer, he would certainly finish whatever work he has started in the Christian. Again, if he always works irresistibly with Christians and finishes the work he begins in them it seems to follow the only reason God works this way in some people and not to others is because, without regard to their faith or works, God has absolutely predestined the people he works with to life eternal. These steps are easy for some Christians to make and believe based on their experience of God working in them in a way which appeared to them they did not have the power to deny God's will in their life.

> While Scripture rightly should shape experience, in much predestinarian exegesis, the texts have become overwhelmed precipitously by this bias in experience. Thus the tables have turned on the charge against pietism, that it is too experientially

---

[22]   Wesley, *Works*, 10:204-59

and emotively oriented, and this charge is now addressed directly to those most prone to make it.[23]

Then Wesley turns to some statements and agreements which Protestant Christians have drawn up and are naturally available for any Christian to read. For instance, he quotes positions of "The Protestant Confession of Faith" which was written in 1559. Also the Dutch in 1618 at Dort drew up a statement which discusses election and reprobation in a positive light.

Again Wesley finds "The Confession of Faith," written by a group of English and Scotch in 1646. This document, also speaks positively about predestination.[24]

Finally he quotes from Calvin's "Institutes of the Christian Religion," showing Calvin believed in and taught election and reprobation which of course is no surprise to us.[25]

Once Wesley has pointed to the several places within the church and our Christian experience where one may find support for the doctrines of election and reprobation, he attacks the problem of those Christians who think they support election but do not or are not so sure with regard to the doctrine of reprobation.

2. SOME CHRISTIANS ARE CONFUSED ABOUT THE LINK BETWEEN ELECTION AND REPROBATION

Wesley reaches out to these Christians, allowing for the sincerity of their beliefs before he begins the discussion of these beliefs.

> "I am verily persuaded, that, in the uprightness of your hearts, you defend the doctrine of unconditional election; even in the same uprightness wherein you reject and abhor that of conditional reprobation. But consider, I intreat you, whether you are consistent with yourselves; consider whether this election can be separate from reprobation; whether one of them

---

23 Oden, *John Wesley's Scriptural Christianity*, 263
24 Wesley, *Works*, 10:206
25 Wesley, *Works*, 10:206

does not imply the other, so that, in holding one, you must hold both.[26]

Wesley says the position of many is both must be held together. In support of this he mentions the decrees he has quoted and Calvin. The quotes given to support Calvin's position are quite devastating to one who would try to straddle the position, holding for election and against reprobation.

> "Many," says he, (Calvin) "as it were to excuse God, own election, and deny reprobation. But this is quite silly and childish. For election cannot stand without reprobation. Whom God passes by, those he reprobates. It is one and the same thing. [Parenthesis mine.][27]

Then Wesley generously says some may not have considered that the two, of necessity, go together. These folks may hold reprobation but are actually not aware of it, because they have not considered deeply enough their own beliefs and the consequences of those beliefs. It is possible upon reflection they will join Calvin and others in the belief of predestination (election and reprobation) or they may decide to abandon predestination altogether.

Wesley asks one question of these Christians and says how they answer the question may clarify things for them. The question is this: Is it possible for a person to be saved who is not elected by God? Or, to put it another way is it possible for one who has not been elected by God to be saved? If the Christian answers either of these questions (really they are both the same) in the negative, such a Christian believes in both election and reprobation.

> Let me intreat you to make this case your own. In the midst of life, you are in death; your soul is dead while you live, if you live in sin, if you do not live to God. And who can deliver you from the body of this death? Only the grace of God in Jesus Christ our Lord. But God hath decreed to give this grace to others only,

---

26   Wesley, *Works*, 10:207
27   Wesley, *Works*, 10:207

and not to you; to leave you in unbelief and spiritual death, and for that unbelief to punish you with death everlasting. Well then mayest thou cry, even till thy throat is dry, "O wretched man that I am!" For an unchangeable, irresistible decree standeth between thee and the very possibility of salvation. Go now and find out how to split the hair between thy being reprobated and not elected; how to separate reprobation, in its most effectual sense, from unconditional election![28]

Wesley can find no way a Christian can believe in either election or reprobation and not be forced to believe in the other as well. He suggests to his reader who has thought he holds election without reprobation they should now agree it is impossible to believe in one and not the other.

Turning to the doctrine itself, Wesley defines it classically. The doctrine is God from before the creation of the world, of his own will and pleasure, determined in a fixed decree for all who would be born from the beginning to the end of the world. This decree is unchangeable with regard to God and is irresistible with regard to man. This decree is that part of mankind will be saved from sin and hell and all the rest of mankind are to perish forever without hope. None of those who have been decreed to perish forever without God's grace given to them will live. God's grace could have prevented them from this death without hope but God chose not to do so in order to show his power and sovereignty over the world.[29]

What about election? Don't the Scriptures talk about election? What happened to the concept of election?

Wesley says he finds two kinds of election in the Scriptures. The first election is when God elects a person or persons to do something in the world. This election Wesley believes is not only personal but it is also absolute and unconditional. The person or persons appointed by God to perform some act or appointed task will perform this act or task.

He points to God using Cyrus to rebuild the temple and the use of Paul to preach the gospel as examples of this type of election. However, this type of election is not equivalent to salvation because Christ told the disciples he chose all of them but one would betray him. Judas was chosen

---

[28] Wesley, *Works*, 10:208
[29] Wesley, *Works*, 10:209

but he was not saved because of Christ's selection or election of him. His behavior after the selection, his betrayal of Christ, was a denial of Christ. He was selected but not saved.

The second type of election Wesley believes in is a divine appointment of some men to eternal happiness. Wesley hastens to say this particular election is not unconditional, nor is it irresistible. This decree of God will not change and men cannot change this decree. Before the predestinarians can say "Ah ha, you believe as we do," Wesley says the eternal decree is those who believe shall be saved and those who do not believe will be damned.

> According to this, all true believers are in Scripture termed elect, as all who continue in unbelief are so long properly reprobates, that is, unapproved of God, and without discernment touching the things of the Spirit.[30]

God sees all things at once; he sees eternity in one view. For example He can call Abraham the "father of many nations" even before Isaac was born. In a similar way God calls all true believers as elect from the foundation of the world, even though they were not actually elect, or believers until many years or generations later. Only in their own time did they become sons of God by faith.

This type of election Wesley understands and affirms. However, he cannot believe in unconditional election because he cannot find it in the Scriptures and he does not believe in unconditional reprobation. He finds such a belief to be irreconcilable with the Scriptures.

Wesley points to many places in Scripture which go against reprobation, many of them state God is willing to save all, others state Christ came to save all and many state about the justice of God.

> Especially if divine sovereignty is the solitary string on one's fiddle, one may tilt toward predestinarian exegesis. But those who seek to understand the intimate inward dialogue of grace and freedom look for a more complex and interactive field theory.[31]

---

[30]   Wesley, *Works*, 10:210
[31]   Oden, *John Wesley's Scriptural Christianity*, 263

3. God's Justice and Reprobation

Some may ask how Wesley's view of reprobation and election do justice to the justice of God. As far as the justice of God is concerned Wesley first says the sovereignty of God never overrides the justice of God.

He believes unconditional reprobation to contradict and indeed to overthrow the justice of God. Yes, says Wesley, God is the judge of the world but how does God's justice judge? How can God justly judge the world if reprobation is true? People cannot be judged for sin because they couldn't help it. Are they then to be judged for what they could not help? Or again, are they to be judged for the sin they were given no forgiving grace to erase? What if they killed themselves to get away from sinning?

> But could they even thus then have escaped from sin? Not without that grace which you suppose God had absolutely determined never to give them. And yet you suppose him to send them into eternal fire, for not escaping from sin! that is, in plain terms, for not having that grace which God had decreed they should never have! O strange justice! What a picture do you draw of the Judge of all the earth!

We could, Wesley says, discuss condemning the reprobates because they are not performing good acts or deeds of mercy. For instance we could say they did not help the poor or feed the hungry or clothe the naked etc. However, the answer is really the same. How could they do these good works if they were not given the power to do them by God's grace? If they did not have the ability to do good works because they are reprobates, how can they be judged for not having what they have not been given? Would the God of justice condemn people for not doing what they did not have the power to do?

Let's discuss inward sins, evil desires, unholy tempers, and vile affections. If the reprobates were able to rescue themselves from these things and yet persisted in them, they indeed would be correctly punished. If however, they were not given the power to rescue themselves from these things how can they be fairly judged for not doing what they couldn't help? "Will God doom that man to the bottomless pit, because of that uncleanness which he could not save himself from, and which God could have saved him from, but would not?"[32] Consider the proposition of a human judge or ruler acting in such a manner today. Wouldn't we think such behavior was awful?

Perhaps the reprobation believer thinks the reprobate should be judged because of his unbelief. This could be the sin which does a man in, couldn't it? The problem with this line of thinking is though it is true they do not believe in Christ, but how could they? The gift of belief is one, according to the reprobationists, God will not give to him. Should God condemn these people because they did not receive the gift he eternally deemed not to give them?

Could it be, as the reprobationist believes, Christ did not die for these who are reprobates? If this were true it is obvious they could never be saved. If saving faith is a sure trust God in Christ loved me and gave himself for me, how could the reprobate believe this unless he is called to believe a lie because he has been preordained to be a reprobate and thus not able to believe or trust that God in Christ died for him?

If God is a just God, there is no way there can be any judgment or even a future condition of rewards or punishments. If there were rewards and punishments and God is to judge each person according to his works, those who seek life by well-doing and trusting in what God has done through Christ receive eternal life. However those who do not obey the truth and who are unrighteous shall receive condemnation.

How can this judgment be true if those who are reprobates are unable to believe and cannot help but do evil and on the other hand those who are elect cannot help but do well? Therefore, in the reprobationist way of thinking God works irresistibly on the elect and Satan works irresistibly on the reprobate. Thus neither of them can help doing what they do because either God or Satan is irresistibly in control of their lives. If man is controlled irresistibly by either God or Satan man cannot be said to be acting at all. If man is not acting at all, other than through the irresistible influence of powers outside himself, how can he correctly be said to receive rewards or punishments for things he could not help or control?

> Justice can have no place in rewarding or punishing mere
> machines, driven to and fro by an external force. So that your

---

[32] Wesley, *Works*, 10:222

supposition of God's ordaining from eternity whatsoever should be done to the end of the world: as well as that of God's acting irresistibly in the elect, and Satan's acting irresistibly in the reprobates; utterly overthrows the Scripture doctrine of rewards and punishments, as well as of a judgment to come.[33]

What can we say then about God's truth? We've talked about how reprobation fits with God's justice, how then does reprobation fit in with God's Truth? It does not fit very well at all, says Wesley. He says contrary to the doctrine of reprobation God has stated three things in the scriptures.

The first is Christ died for all. He finds this in II Corinthians 5:14. He believes all of us are dead in sin and Christ died to take away the sin from all of us, not just some of us. He asks for those who believe in predestination to show him the scriptures where it states Christ did not die for all but for a select few. This would indeed put limits upon the great acts God has performed through Christ on the cross.

The second is Christ is the propitiation for the sins of the whole world (I John 2:2) and not just for a part of the world or some select group. Again, what Scriptures say Jesus is not the propitiation for the sins of the whole world but he is the propitiation for the sins of only some? This would be another case of extremely limiting God's works.

The third is Christ died for all men so they should live for him (II Corinthians 5:15) and by so doing they are saved from their sins. This is the reason Christ died. Also, where does it say in scripture Christ died for some men but not for all?

Again, how does the doctrine of reprobation square with God's love? We have found reprobation does not agree with God's justice or his truth, but what about God's love? This is the attribute which we think of above all others when we think about God is that God is love. His love even goes out to those who do not return his love. He is good even to those who are evil and are not thankful for his love. God's love knows no bounds.

The truth and sincerity of God are called into question if Christ did not die for all but only for a few. How can God and Christ be sincere when they give the great commission to offer God's grace to all if part of

---

33   Wesley, Works, 10:224

mankind from the foundation of the world has been set aside and made unable to accept God's offer?[34]

Let's look closely at how God's love relates to the person who has not been elected or who is reprobated. You can't say the reprobated person is an object of love or the goodness of God because God has created him only to die apart from him. Surely one cannot think God's goodness is concerned with the redemption of the reprobate. Such a thought would obviously be a contradiction in terms. How can God want to redeem the reprobate when he has created him from before the creation of the world to die apart from God? This thought would make no sense at all.

So God can give good to all men, even the reprobate, but in being good to him and allowing him to enjoy these goods God still withholds himself and thereby salvation from the reprobate. This person has no saving grace because God has withheld it from him. Any grace at all given to him was not given in order to save him because he is eternally damned by being reprobated (not elected for salvation).

Wesley asks how this person who has not received saving grace but instead has received damning grace, is representative of God's love. Is this the kind of love you want? Is this the kind of love you can believe in and respond to?

> Can you think, that the loving, the merciful God, ever dealt thus with any soul which he hath made? But you must and do believe this, if you believe unconditional election. For it holds reprobation in its bosom; they never were, never can be, divided. Take then your choice. If, for the sake of election, you will swallow reprobation, well. But, if you cannot digest this, you must necessarily give up unconditional election.[35]

4. CONFUSION ABOUT MAN'S FREE WILL

What about free-will? What is free-will? Is it possible to have free-will and believe in election and/or reprobation? In speaking of free will we are discussing it in religious terms having to do with the salvation of man and not whether I will purchase a coke or candy bar.

---

[34] Wesley, *Works*, 10:227
[35] Wesley, *Works*, 10:229

Some believe if they do not hold to the doctrine of election they must believe in free-will and by so believing, they rob God of his glory in the salvation of man. They think if men are not elected by God somehow God's glory is lost. Wesley contends there are many who believe in election and yet who utterly deny the consequence of their belief. They then do not allow even natural free-will in man because they think it is repugnant to God's glory.

> So the Assembly of Divines, (and therein the body of Calvinists both in England and Scotland,) "God hath endued the will of man with that natural liberty that is neither forced, nor, by an absolute necessity of nature, determined to do good or evil." (Chap. ix.:) And this they assert of man in his fallen state even before he receives the grace of God.[36]

Wesley says there are some people who believe in election and also believe in free-will and they do not see the conflict in their thinking. It is important for us to know Wesley thinks the definition of free-will as described above is incorrect. He believes this definition goes too far, at least in the moral realm. He does not believe man has a natural free-will. Free-will is not something man naturally has; rather, free-will is the gift of God.

But some will say if man has the power of free-will then God cannot receive the absolute glory for saving man because God alone is not then totally responsible for man's salvation. They assert if man works with God to work out his own salvation then God does not do the whole work because man is working with God. It is obviously true if man can work out his own salvation with God, God does not do the whole work. God can still have all the glory for man's salvation because it is God himself who has given man the power to work with him. Since this is a work of God's grace and since we could not work with God for our salvation unless God gave us the power to do so, and we selected to do so, it is God's work, and therefore all of the glory does belong to God.

Wesley even allows Christian experience to play a part in the discussion at this point. Don't most of us have experiences in which we could have

---

[36] Wesley, *Works*, 10:229

easily made the wrong choice? We were very tempted to choose the wrong way but something happened and we yielded to God and instead chose the correct way.

> Has not even experience taught you this? Have you not often felt, in a particular temptation, power either to resist or yield to the grace of God? And when you have yielded to "work together with Him," did you not find it very possible, notwithstanding, to give him all the glory? So that both experience and Scripture are against you here, and make it clear to every impartial inquirer, that though man has freedom to work or not "work together with God," yet may God have the whole glory of his salvation.[37]

Lest some think Wesley believes the glory of our salvation should not be given to God alone, he says he gives God alone the glory. If, however, one says God alone performs the whole work, this is a different matter, but the true answer is not quite so simple. In one sense it is God alone who works. For example Wesley believes it is the work of God alone to justify, to sanctify, and to glorify us. These three concepts comprise the total of man's salvation.

This is not to say man can only resist God and cannot work together with God or God's work is the sum and total of our salvation so man's participation is totally excluded. The objection of some at this point seems to be that man's salvation must be due to an irresistible power of God so as to totally exclude any work or effort by man. Wesley does not believe God's grace is irresistible in the sense man cannot refuse or deny God's grace.

The question Wesley asks to those who say man cannot play a part in his salvation is in what way is it more to the glory of God—to save man by God's irresistible grace or by a free agent who can either resist or concur with God's loving grace?

While we are considering this what is the glory of God we are talking about? Wesley finds two uses of the term. The first is God's essence and his attributes. These are the same yesterday, today, and tomorrow. They do not increase or decrease because they are forever the same. The second use of the glory of God in the Scripture is the manifestation of his essential glory,

---

[37] Wesley, *Works*, 10:230

eternal power, and Godhead, and also his attributes, especially his justice, mercy, and truth. Man cannot help or work with God in the first meaning but he can work with God in the second meaning. The first is what God is and the second is how each part of God's glory manifests itself to us.

Wesley's point again is this: are God's glorious attributes, especially his justice, mercy, and truth better manifested if God irresistibly saves man by giving man no choice in the matter, or if we are saved by the grace God gives us to either resist this grace or agree and work with it? Wesley says those who believe in reprobation must believe it is more glorious for man to be saved irresistibly, which again means man has no choice in the matter.

If man is saved by irresistible grace, man becomes in effect a machine, only able to do what God irresistibly does in him and the end result of this approach is man now has therefore been successfully removed from any possible rewards or punishments.

> Wesley held to the freewill defense that God creates freedom, and freedom chooses evil in its own struggle against God, who is the author not of sin but of freedom, which is created good even if prone to fall. No creature capable of mirroring the image of God can be considered an automaton.
>
> Human beings are created to reflect the freedom of God. Only through freedom can the goodness of God be consciously and rationally reflected, unlike inorganic matter, which can only refract God's goodness inertly, without speech or reason.[38]

Wesley asks us to look at some of the attributes, especially God's wisdom, justice, and love, and see whether free-will as he believes it or reprobation, as he does not, is the better fit.

The wisdom of God is great indeed if the "true light which enlightens everyone" sets before us life and death, good and evil. God is willing for all men to be saved but he is not willing to force men to be saved. God is willing to save all men but he is not willing to save them as inanimate objects or machines without any choice or say in the matter. God prefers to save men as reasonable creatures who have some ability to discover what is good and the ability to accept or refuse this grace of God.

---

[38]   Oden, *John Wesley's Scriptural Christianity*, 269

God works in many small ways to bring man to him besides the general knowledge of good and evil. God may offer many secret reproofs if man acts contrary to what is good. Wesley thinks God may gently woo us to get us to walk in the light.

In this way God works with all men, even with those who have no knowledge of his written Word, our Scriptures. What great wisdom God shows if man possesses some degree of freedom of choice for God or against him.

God first provides the light for our feet, the way for us to accept and go with the strongest sanctions of life and death. God tries every way to reach for the souls of men. Sometimes he does this through their understandings by showing them the folly of their sins. Other times he may work through their affections attacking their lack of gratitude, by gently saying "what more could I have done for you than I have already done?" Then there can be threats such as "unless you repent, you will all perish just as did the Galileans whose blood Pilate had mingled with their sacrifices."

> Now, what wisdom is seen in all this, if man may indeed choose life or death! But if every man be unalterably consigned to heaven or hell before he comes from his mother's womb, where is the wisdom of thio of dealing with him, in every respect, as if he were free, when it is no such thing? What avails, what can this whole dispensation of God avail a reprobate? What are promises or threats, expostulations or reproofs to thee thou firebrand of hell? What, indeed, (O my brethren, suffer me to speak, for I am full of matter!) but empty farce, but mere grimace, sounding words, that mean just nothing? O where (to wave all other considerations now) is the wisdom of this proceeding! To what end does all this apparatus serve? If you say, "To insure his damnation," alas, what needeth that, seeing this was insured before the foundation of the world! Let mankind then judge, which of these accounts is more for the glory of God's wisdom![39]

So much for the wisdom of God now what about God's justice? If man really is capable of choosing good or evil then man can properly be

---

[39]   Wesley, *Works*, 10:233

a recipient of God's justice. God's justice will then usher forth in rewards and punishments. If, however, man is a machine or like a stone which has no choice, he cannot be a proper recipient of God's justice and receive rewards or punishments for these things over which he has no power.

If man cannot but sin because he has not received the grace of God because God has eternally decreed he is not to receive this grace, man has no power or ability to do anything but sin. Such a God Wesley maintains is not the Christian God. The Christian God is just in all his ways.

> This is not the God of the Christians. Our God is just in all his ways; he repeath not where he hath not strewed. He requireth only according to what he hath given; and where he hath given little, little is required. The glory of his justice is this, to "reward every man according to his works." Hereby is that glorious attribute shown, evidently set forth before men and angels, in that it is accepted of every man according to that he hath and not according to that he hath not. This is that just decree which cannot pass, either in time of in eternity.[40]

If man has the free-will to deny God or to accept God working in him, God's justice is given full scope and power. If, however, man does not have free-will and cannot accept or reject God's grace then God's justice is truncated into nonexistence

We have discussed God's wisdom and justice, now what about God's love? If God's love is fixed only on a few without regard for the bulk of the human race, if God says I will save the one and let the ninety-nine go without mercy, how does this show God's love? If one says in reply God does it because he does it and this is his will, what would we say about a person who had the power to help thousands or hundreds or tens of people but chose to help only one or two? And on top of this when he was questioned about why he let so many die when he could have easily saved them, he said to the TV crew "I won't save them because I won't "or "I didn't because I didn't." What would we say about such a person, Governor, President, etc?

---

40   Wesley, *Works*, 10:234

Someone may say God's love is shown better by irresistibly saving some (the elect) than it would be by giving the choice of salvation to all men and actual salvation to all who choose it. Wesley will not buy this argument.

> I appeal to every impartial mind, whether the reverse be not obviously true; whether the mercy of God would not be far less gloriously displayed, in saving a few by his irresistible power, and leaving all the rest without help, without hope, to perish everlastingly, than in offering salvation to every creature, actually saving all that consent thereto, and doing for the rest all that infinite wisdom, almighty power, and boundless love can do, without forcing them to be saved, which would be to destroy the very nature that he had given them I appeal, I say, to every impartial mind, and to your own, if not quite blinded with prejudice, which of these accounts places the mercy of God in the most advantageous light.[41]

These three, wisdom, justice and love have been discussed, but what about God's sovereignty? How does God's sovereignty fit in with this discussion? Wesley sees the sovereignty of God in many aspects, the first is "In fixing from eternity that decree touching the sons of men, 'He that believeth shall be saved. He that believeth not shall be damned.'"[42] Wesley also sees God's sovereignty in the general circumstances of creation such as the time, the place, and how God created everything, in giving the natural endowments men possess, the birth of us all, and in giving to us the gifts of the Spirit.

To make sure we do not go too far Wesley quickly says God's sovereignty does not apply to disposing of the eternal states of man. The eternal states of man are determined by a combination of the attributes including His sovereignty but also his justice, mercy, and truth.

God receives no pleasure in the death of the wicked; he would prefer they turn from their wicked ways. Wesley refers to quotes Ezekiel 33:ll, "Say to them, As I live, says the Lord God, I have no pleasure in the death of the wicked, but that the wicked turn from their ways and live; turn back, turn back from your evil ways: for why would you die, O house of

---

41 Wesley, *Works*, 10:235
42 Wesley, *Works*, 10:235

Israel?(NRSV)" Thus we see God, rather than deciding from eternity who are the elect and who are reprobated, here we hear God say he prefers for the evil men to live by turning from their ways.

As for the unchangeableness of God, before someone misunderstand what he is saying about God's unchangeableness, Wesley hastens to explain he means God is unchangeable in his decrees. Not just any decrees of God either, but those given in the words "He that believeth shall be saved: he that believeth not shall be damned."[43]

Wesley also thinks God is unchangeable in his love and hatred, but what does he mean by this? We find he is consistent with the rest of his teachings.

> God unchangeably loveth righteousness, and hateth iniquity. Unchangeably he loveth faith, and unchangeably hateth unbelief. In consequence hereof he unchangeably loves the righteous, and hateth the workers of iniquity. He unchangeably loves them that believe, and hates willful, obstinate unbelievers. So that the scripture account of God's unchangeableness with regard to his decrees, is this? He has unchangeably decreed to save holy believers, and to condemn obstinate, impenitent unbelievers. And according to Scripture, his unchangeableness of affection properly and primarily regards tempers and not persons; and persons (as Enoch, Noah, Abraham) only as those tempers are found in them. Let then the unchangeableness of God be put upon the right foot; let the Scripture be allowed to fix the objects of it, and it will as soon prove transubstantiation, as unconditional election.[44]

It is in this way Wesley relates God's unchangeableness to our discussion of election and reprobation.

Now, how about the faithfulness of God? Wesley places the faithfulness of God as a part of God's truth, i.e. whatever God says he will do he will do. His promises are sure because God is faithful in his performance of them.

---

[43] Wesley, *Works*, 10:238
[44] Wesley, *Works*, 10:238

To who are God's promises made? They are made to Abraham and his seed. Thus it is those who, like Abraham, believe in God, to them are God's promises made. Because God has made these gospel promises he will be faithful to them.

This is the covenant with which Wesley would agree. He will have no part of another covenant he has heard of in which God the Father and God the Son agree for the Son to suffer various things and die and because of the Son's work the Father will give the Son so many souls. These souls only will be saved and the others will be damned. Wesley does not find any Scripture to back this second idea which he finds active in his day.

The covenant Wesley agrees to and finds Scriptural is "The grand covenant which we allow to be mentioned therein, is a covenant between God and man, established in the hands of a Mediator, 'who tasted death for every man,' and thereby purchased it for all the children of men. The tenor of it (so often mentioned already) is this: 'Whosoever believeth unto the end, so as to show his faith by his works, I the Lord will reward that soul eternally. But whosoever will not believe, and consequently dieth in his sins, I will punish him with everlasting destruction.'"[45]

The meaning of this covenant is whoever believes to the end and shows his faith in God by his works, the Lord will give to such a person eternal life. The reverse is also true, whoever does not believe and who therefore dies in his sin will not receive eternal life but will receive eternal destruction. Charles Wesley says it so well:

> Ah! Gentle, gracious Dove;
> And art Thou grieved in me,
> That sinners should restrain Thy love,
> And say, "It is not free;
> It is not free for *all*";
> The *most* Thou *past by*,
> And mockest with a fruitless call
> Whom Thou hast doom'd to die.
>
> They think Thee *not sincere*
> In giving each his day:
> *"Thou only draws'st the sinner near.*

---

[45]   Wesley, *Works*, 10:239

To cast him quite away.
To aggravate his sin.
His sure damnation seal,
Thou Show'st him Heaven, and say'st go in—
And thrusts him into Hell.

O horrible decree,
Worthy of whence it came!
Forgive their hellish blasphemy
Who charge it on the Lamb,
Those pity Him inclined
To leave His throne above,
The Friend and Saviour of mankind,
The God of grace and love . . . [46]

A good place to look in order to study this covenant experience is to look closely at the covenant God made with Abraham. By looking at this covenant we can learn something about all God's covenants with man.

The first covenant is found in Genesis 15:18, "On that day the Lord made a covenant with Abram, saying, 'to your descendants I give this land . . .'" However a better description of the covenant is found in Genesis 17:1-14 (NRSV).

When Abram was ninety-nine years old, the Lord appeared to Abram, and said to him, "I am God Almighty; walk before me, and be blameless. And I will make my covenant between me and you, and will make you exceedingly numerous." Then Abram fell on his face: and God said to him, "As for me, this is my covenant with you: You shall be the ancestor of a multitude of nations. No longer shall you name be Abram, but your name shall be Abraham; for I have made you the ancestor of a multitude of nations. I will make you exceedingly fruitful; and I will make nations of you, and kings shall come from you. I will establish my covenant between me and you, and your offspring after you throughout their generations, for an everlasting covenant, to be God to you and to your offspring after you. And I will give to you, and to your offspring after

---

[46]   Tyson, *Assist Me to Proclaim*, 111-12

you, the land where you are now an alien, all the land of Canaan, for a perpetual holding; and I will be their God."

God said to Abraham, "As for you, you shall keep my covenant, you and your offspring and after you throughout their generations. This is my covenant, which you shall keep, between me and you and your offspring after you: Every male among you shall be circumcised. You shall circumcise the flesh of your foreskins, and it shall be a sign of the covenant between me and you. Throughout your generations every male among you shall be circumcised when he is eight days old, including the slave born in your house and the one bought with your money from any foreigner who is not of your offspring. Both the slave born in your house and the one bought with your money must be circumcised. So shall my covenant be in your flesh an everlasting covenant. Any uncircumcised male who is not circumcised in the flesh of his foreskin shall be cut off from his people; he has broken my covenant."

From his reading of this Scripture Wesley concludes this original covenant was both everlasting and conditional. This covenant is also discussed by Paul in his letter to the Romans (4:3ff). Further explanation is also found in Genesis 18:17-19 "The Lord said, 'Shall I hide from Abraham what I am about to do, seeing that Abraham shall become a great and mighty nation, and all the nations of the earth shall be blessed in him? No, for I have chosen him, that he may charge his children and his household after him to keep the way of the Lord by doing righteousness and justice; so that the Lord may bring about for Abraham what he has promised him.'" (NRSV) Here God says he will perform his part of the covenant. An even clearer account is found in Genesis 22:16-18 in which God says "because" Abraham has done certain things and "because" Abraham has followed God's will, God will perform.

Later to the people in Moses' day, God gave the Ten Commandments as the terms of the covenant. As we know, the people rebelled and worshipped a golden calf and God declares (Lev. 26:3-46) if the people walk in God's way he will be their God and they will be his people. If they break the covenant he will go against them. If then the people return to God's way he will remember the covenant and they will be in the covenant relationship again.

5. Christians May Fall

We could spend a lot of time on this point if we wish, but even with experience we will not be able to prove very much. The only thing Wesley thinks we can prove is the patience of God. He does not want any of us to die. God puts up with a lot of man's foolishness and sinfulness, and wants to bring us back to him. Experience cannot give us the answer about whether or not those who were once in a saving relationship can fall.

Wesley quotes from Ezekiel to show true believers or those who God judges to be holy or righteous may fall. "But when the righteous turn away from their righteousness and commit iniquity and do the same abominable things that the wicked do, shall they live? None of the righteous deeds that they have done shall be remembered; for the treachery of which they are guilty and the sin they have committed, they shall die." (Ezekiel 18:24 NRSV) With a full reading of this chapter we can see the righteousness spoken of here indeed is the righteousness which is inward. Likewise the death spoken of here is eternal death not a supposition or some other meaning. The person who is at one time righteous in the eyes of God may yet fall from grace. Wesley goes through a list of conditions in which men may be in their relationship to God. He has several points to consider, all of them showing at whatever step or relationship man may have with God, man may still fall from grace.

The first question may be asked in covenantal terms is: aren't all those who have been in the covenant relationship with God assured of staying in that covenant relationship? Wesley thinks this is a very human thought and one we would like to believe, even though it is untrue.

The second consideration is about a man who has the faith which produces a good conscience may fall. He finds support for this in Timothy (I Timothy 1:18-19).

The third point is even those who have been grafted into the tree or the church may also fall. Support for this is found in Romans 11:19-22. These people were grafted into the olive tree which is the invisible church and yet it is possible for them to be cut off from the church and it is further possible they may not be grafted in again.

Wesley's fourth point is some who are branches of Christ and the true vine may yet fall and become separated from the saving relationship. Wesley finds support for this point in John 15:1-7. In this case Wesley points out these people were in Christ, a part of the true vine, some branches did not abide in Christ so they were cast forth or out of the church and were not grafted in again. They were cast into the fire and burned. So, true believers who are branches of the true vine may fall.

His fifth point is people who know Christ and by this knowledge have escaped the sins or defilements of the world and its pollutants may yet fall back and perish forever. Wesley finds support for this position in II Peter 2:20-21.

His sixth is even some who see the light of the glory of God in the face of Jesus Christ and who have had the gift of the Holy Spirit, and have from this experience the witness and fruits of the Spirit, even these may fall and perish forever. Wesley's support is found in Hebrews 6:4-6. Here we have true believers who have fallen.

Seventh is those who live by faith may also fall away from God. The support for this is Hebrews 10:38.

> "The just" (the justified person, of whom only this can be said) "shall live by faith;" even now shall live the life which is hid with Christ in God; and if he endure unto the end, shall live with God forever. "But if any man draw back," saith the Lord, "my soul shall have no pleasure in him;" that is, I will utterly cast him off: And accordingly the drawing back here spoken of, is termed in the verse immediately following, "drawing back to perdition."[47]

Eighth is even those who are sanctified by the blood of the covenant may fall and perish. (Hebrews 10:26-29) Sanctification or Christian perfection will be covered in another chapter so we will not discuss it at this time. Wesley says it is plain to him from the Scripture "(1) That the person mentioned here was once sanctified by the blood of the covenant. (2) That he afterward, by known, willful sin, trod under foot the Son of God. And, (3) That he hereby incurred a sorer punishment than death; namely, death everlasting."[48]

---

[47] Wesley, *Works*, 10:249
[48] Wesley, *Works*, 10:252

This makes Wesley's theology a very dynamic one. Things are not a once and for all, there can be change at any time. We must be ever vigilant and work continually with God and not forget Him.

Does the message of these points make salvation unconditional? Wesley says he does not say salvation is conditional or unconditional there, but he does state what he finds in the Scriptures. Wesley believes the possibility of salvation has been bought for everyone and is actually given to those who believe. He says, "If you call this conditional salvation, God made it so from the beginning of the world; and he hath declared it so to be, at sundry times and in divers manners; of old by Moses and the Prophets, and in later times by Christ and his Apostles."[49]

Then Wesley says those who believe in reprobation believe a doctrine which is not only unsupported by Scriptures but is contrary to both reason and Scripture.

The only thing which humbles man is not one opinion or another opinion which man holds. What humbles man is the love of God, and only the love of God. This love shows man what he really is and that he cannot hide himself or his sins from this loving God.

6. THE GRAND OBJECTION TO REPROBATION

"This is my grand objection to the doctrine of reprobation, or (which is the same) unconditional election. That it is an error, I know; because, if this were true, the whole Scripture must be false. But it is not only for this—because it is an error—that I so earnestly oppose it, but because it is an error of so pernicious consequence to the souls of men; because it directly and naturally tends to hinder the inward work of God in every stage of it."[50]

Wesley uses an example to further his cause. If we find a man in sin and we exhort him to change, repent, and turn away from sin to Christ this man may tell us "what must be must be." "If I am of the elect, I must be saved and if I am not of the elect I won't be saved."

Do we know a person who is lukewarm, who is really not working as a Christian or trying to live his life with God? If we try to stir him up to

---

[49] Wesley, *Works*, 10:254
[50] Wesley, *Works*, 10:256

care about his own salvation and he appears not to respond we can tell him he must desire salvation in order to be saved. He may respond to us if he is one of the elect, God will make him willing at the right time, but if he is not of the elect there is nothing he can do to change the decree.

Wesley sees examples everyday of those who have begun well and had faith in God and His Son only to lose all this because of the unscriptural doctrine of election and reprobation.

Again, Christ died for everybody and God wants all men to be saved. To those who think they can wait awhile and sin awhile longer, Wesley says this kind of thinking does not come from his position. It does however arise from the thinking of those who believe Christ died only for the elect. Those folks have every reason to say they can wait awhile longer and sin awhile longer because if they are one of the elect God will make sure they change in time and if they are reprobated it wouldn't make any difference no matter what they did.

Because Wesley believes strongly in the Christian life of holiness the doctrine of predestination is abhorrent to him. He knew the Christian life should show fruits of that life and the way of Scriptural holiness was the only life for a Christian. The wait and see position is opposed to the active holiness seeking position of Wesley.

> . . . although the continental reformers and Wesley all assented to a doctrine of total depravity, the basic contours of their theologies remain distinct, due to different conceptions of grace. Wesley's doctrine of prevenient grace allows him to hold together, without any contradiction, the four motifs of total depravity, salvation by grace, human responsibility, and the offer of salvation to all. The theologies of Calvin and Luther, on the other hand, can only hold the first two motifs together, and their doctrines of predestination and election explain why all will not be saved.[51]

---

[51] Collins, *The Scriptural Way of Salvation*, 45

7. Free Grace

Wesley, as we can see, is a proponent of free grace and this free grace is available for all. The grace Wesley speaks of is grace not earned by any means which man can contrive. This grace is free. This grace is not given only to some either, it is given to every man.

> The grace or love of God, whence cometh our salvation, is FREE IN ALL, and FREE FOR ALL. First. It is free IN ALL to whom It is given. It does not depend on any power or merit in man: no, not in any degree, neither in whole, nor in part. It does not in anywise depend either on the good works or righteousness of the receiver; not on anything he has done, or anything he is. It does not depend on his endeavours. It does not depend on his good tempers, or good desires, or good purposes and intentions; for all these flow from the free grace of God; they are the streams only, not the fountain. They are the fruits of free grace, and not the root. They are not the cause, but the effects of it. Whatsoever good is in man, or is done by man, God is the author and doer of it. Thus is his grace free in all; that is, no way depending on any power or merit in man, but on God alone, who freely gave us his own Son, and "with him freely giveth us all things."[52]

The point Wesley uses in his sermon on "Free Grace" was accepted by him years later as still good. He did not here call it prevenient grace but some of the grace under discussion obviously was prevenient grace.

The first problem is if you believe in predestination there is no need for preaching. This conclusion is obvious. Either you are predetermined to be saved or damned. In either case there is no need for you to attend the services and listen to the sermon because it will make no difference in the final analysis. If it makes no difference whether you listen or not one of the ordinances of God has been made void and this cannot be true if God is God and not divided against himself.

The second problem is predestination destroys the need for holiness which to Wesley is the goal of the ordinances of God. By believing you are

---

[52] Wesley, *Works*, 7:373-4

saved or damned and nothing you or anybody else can do to change this decree then there is no motive to seek holiness in this life.

Such things as meekness and loving our neighbor—our neighbor who is evil and not thankful for anything done for him—are then without a reason for us to pursue such a difficult life. Why should we bother to extend ourselves when to do so counts for nothing?

Try as you may it is difficult for you if you are one of the elect—you are one of the elect, aren't you—to keep from looking down at those who you can tell by looking at their life are not one of the elect. You are not supposed to look down at them but how can you avoid it—you being one of the elect and they obviously not being one of the elect?

> But you cannot help sometimes applying your general doctrine to particular persons: The enemy of souls will apply it for you. You know how often he has done so. But you rejected the thought with abhorrence. True; as soon as you could; but how did it sour and sharpen your spirit in the mean time! You well know it was not the spirit of love which you then felt towards that poor sinner, whom you supposed or suspected, whether you would or no, to have been hated of God from eternity.[53]

The third problem is the joy and comfort which religion of the heart should bring us is lacking in those who believe in predestination. This is particularly true of those who are reprobated or who think they might be reprobates.

Think of the great promises God has given to mankind and which are found in the scriptures. All of these are lost to you because you might be reprobated by God. These promises are wonderful but they are not for you, they are for others to whom God has been pleased to give the blessing.

Even for those who have been elected or who believe they have been elected there can be problems. You may feel God at work in your life and may know God's spirit is alive in you. However even though you find God alive in you now, you do not have a guarantee you will persevere and finally claim the crown. Lots of folks have started well only to fall before they have finished the race.

---

53   Wesley, *Works*, 7:377

That assurance of faith which these enjoy excludes all doubt and fear. It excludes all kinds of doubt and fear concerning their future perseverance: though it is not properly, as was said before, an assurance of what is future, but only of what *now* is. And this needs not for its support a speculative belief, that whoever is once ordained to life must live; for it is wrought from hour to hour, by the mighty power of God, "by the Holy Ghost which is given unto them." And therefore that doctrine is not of God, because it tends to obstruct, if not destroy, this great work of the Holy Ghost, whence flows the chief comfort of religion, the happiness of Christianity.[54]

The fourth problem is the doctrine of predestination tends to limit or obstruct our desire for holiness of life and the good works we find in the Christian life. Those who are saved may tend to look down on those who they believe are reprobated and thus they are not induced to help them or try to bring them to the Christian life.

If they are damned anyway and you are saved anyway, why should you go out of your way to feed the hungry, or clothe the naked?

It makes no difference to you. You are saved already and they are damned already so nothing you do can help or change the situation.

In either case, your advice, reproof, or exhortation is as needless and useless as our preaching. It is needless to them that are elected; for they will infallibly be saved without it. It is useless to them that are not elected; for with or without it they will infallibly be damned; therefore you cannot consistently with your principles take any pains about their salvation. Consequently, those principles directly tend to destroy your zeal for good works; for all good works; but particularly the greatest of all, the saving of souls from death.[55]

The fifth problem is it is bad enough for holiness, happiness, and good works to be so limited or dropped as we have seen, but predestination also tends to limit or do away with the Christian revelation itself.

---

[54] Wesley, *Works*, 7:378
[55] Wesley, *Works*, 7:379

Some of the writers of the day, who are deists and enjoy putting forward the strengths of man and his lack of need for God, would be happy with this conclusion. The gospel then becomes absolutely unnecessary since there is nothing anybody can do about whether they have been eternally saved or damned.

You can also look at it one way and you can say the gospel is unnecessary, as we have seen. The sixth problem is that we can then put forward the proposition the gospel or revelation contradicts itself. For instance, these believers say when God says He loved Jacob and hated Esau, they take it literally but such interpretation as this does not fit with a God of love.

Many other passages could likewise be cited against each other such as Jesus as the Savior of the world who died for all our sins, etc. Then you can ask why are not all men saved and you are given the answer of predestination.

> Thus manifestly does this doctrine tend to overthrow the whole Christian Revelation, by making it contradict itself; by giving such an interpretation of some texts, as flatly contradicts all the other texts, and indeed the whole scope and tenor of Scripture;—an abundant proof that it is not of God.[56]

The seventh problem Wesley has with predestination as against free grace is it is full of blasphemy. What Wesley is talking about here is everywhere in the scriptures Jesus is calling everyone to come to him. Yet in the doctrine of predestination, we find from the foundation of the world only some can be allowed to be saved. Jesus calls all men knowing in advance only some can answer because those who do not answer are not one of those selected to be saved.

Another example we have is the story of Jesus saying to Jerusalem he would often have gathered her children together but they would not. Jesus saying he would have liked to gather the children of Israel to himself and yet knowing only some will be saved seems to Wesley to be a great contradiction. Quite a contrast is shown here.

> This is the blasphemy clearly contained in *the horrible decree* of predestination! And here I fix my foot. On this I join issue with

---

[56] Wesley, *Works*, 7:381

every assertor of it. You represent God as worse than the devil; more false, more cruel, more unjust. But you say you will prove it by Scripture. Hold! What will you prove by Scripture? that God is worse than the devil? It cannot be. Whatever that Scripture proves, it never can prove this; whatever its true meaning be, this cannot be its true meaning. Do you ask, "What is its true meaning then?" If I say, "I know not," you have gained nothing; for there are many scriptures the true sense whereof neither you nor I shall know till death is swallowed up in victory. But this I know, better it were to say it had no sense at all, than to say it had such a sense as this. It cannot mean, whatever it means besides, that the God of truth is a liar. Let it mean what it will, it cannot mean that the Judge of all the world is unjust. No scripture can mean that God is not love, or that his mercy is not over all his works; that is, whatever it prove beside, no scripture can prove predestination.[57]

Wesley does say there was a decree from before the foundation of the world but it was not predestination. This decree is God has set before men life and death or a blessing and a curse. Those who choose life will have it and those who choose death will have it also—man's will, not God's.

8. CHRISTIANS SHOULD BE UNITED

Wesley admits he may not have changed all opinions to agree with him with regard to the doctrine of predestination which includes election and reprobation. However, since we all believe the scriptures that without holiness no man shall see God; can't we all join together in espousing the main nature of holiness and together talk and agree to seek its necessity?

> As far as is possible, let us join in destroying the works of the devil, and in setting up the kingdom of God upon earth, in promoting righteousness, peace, and joy in the Holy Spirit.
> Of whatever opinion or denomination we are, we must serve either God or the devil. If we serve God, our agreement is far greater than our difference. Therefore, so as far as may be, setting aside that difference, let us unite in destroying the

---

57   Wesley, *Works*, 7:383

works of the devil, in bringing all we can from the power of darkness into the kingdom of God's dear Son. And let us assist each other to value more and more the glorious grace whereby we stand and daily grow in that grace and in the knowledge of our Lord Jesus Christ.[58]

---

[58]   Wesley, *Works*, 10:259

3

GOOD WORKS, ACTIVE HOLINESS AND MEANS OF GRACE

When Wesley was on his way to America the ship he was sailing on got into several powerful storms which had all of those on board fearful for their lives except for a few who were Germans and were of the Moravian Church. When everybody else was afraid and calling out in fear for their lives the Moravians were quiet and peaceful. Wesley himself was fearful for his life. At one point the main-sail split and water poured in between decks. The English screamed but the Germans kept singing hymns. When Wesley asked if they were not afraid they replied they were not afraid to die, even their women and children.

This experience with the Lutheran Moravians and his encounters with them later developed a kinship and a desire to know more about them. Their influence on the early Wesley was strong and he felt close to them. When he got back to England from his time in America he even went to Germany to learn more about them.

The problems, differences, and difficulties between the Moravians and Wesley were slow in arising. It took a lot for Wesley to enter into war with them. It is too bad the split had to come between them but once the problems were engaged there was no turning back for Wesley.

It seemed for awhile the Wesleyan Revival and the Moravians would be able to work together perhaps at locations such as the Fetter-Lane Society which would have had a Moravian and Anglican mixture. However such a joint venture did not happen. Gradually Wesley became more disturbed by some of the beliefs and practices of the Moravians and thus various points of theology began to come into conflict.

These theological differences received an extra push when Philip Molther came to England and began working in locations such as the Fetter-Lane Society. Count Zinzendorf, who was the leader of the Moravians then, also became a problem for Wesley. The split when it comes is not easy. Try as they can it became evident the two cannot peacefully coexist without causing a great deal of confusion and anger among the people they are serving.

This theological war is fought along several fronts, some more serious than others. The areas under discussion are the definition of faith, and also how one is to seek or wait for faith which involves the use or non use of the means of grace. Additionally, there is a problem of whether or not everyone is going to be saved (a form of universal salvation).

The definition of faith also leads into a discussion of justification and sanctification. It centers on the concept of faith; whether there can be a weak and strong faith or if there is really only a strong faith. If one believes there is only one faith, Wesley disagrees because he sees degrees of faith. The Christian life becomes involved because of the quietism of the Moravians in which they do not believe one should use the means of grace to seek God and faith in Christ's work of salvation for us. They also do not think one seeking faith should perform good works towards others because it could be confused with believing in a salvation by works. I think the start of the war began with the issue of quietism and the non use of the sacraments and the war escalated from there. The downplaying of the Lord's Supper is impossible for Wesley to accept. This friction accelerated until the war broke out.

Molther is an advocate of "stillness" which goes against the Wesley grain as a theologian, a practicing Christian, and his personality. Molther is quite different in approach from Peter Bohler and he and Wesley soon begin to have differences which rise to the point they eventually became irreconcilable. These differences cause Wesley to leave the Fetter-Lane Society along with those who chose to follow him, and to the create his own United Society. One of those who sent with Wesley at this time was the Countess of Huntingdon.

Several questions at this time cause the break between the two camps. One of these questions which creates a fuss in the Society is do you seek faith by using all of the means of grace and then use them because you have faith, or do you quietly wait for God to give you the required faith? Another question which is debated is are we to perform good works after faith or are we not responsible for good works because to do so is an attempt to earn your salvation by them? The question of whether justification and sanctification are the same or different and does it really make a difference whether we accept one or the other, come into play here also.

After giving a long time of discussion with the Moravians and careful consideration of the likenesses and differences Wesley comes to the conclusion the differences are too great and serious enough they could not work together.

In various places Wesley lists these three reasons or problems he has with the Moravians. The other problems arose principally through his dealings with one or more Moravians who had views which differed from the Moravian Church. The Moravian Church also later cleaned up some of its thinking and thus removed some of the problems between them and Wesley.

We must remember Wesley knew the Church at a particular period of time and closely knew some of its adherents. We dare not tarnish the whole Moravian Church with all of the things Wesley brought out as problems because as has been said, many of them were the misguided conceptions of a few.

First, they believe in universal salvation. They believed in the final analysis because Christ died for all our sins everyone will be saved. This is quite different from the problem with the Calvinists who believe only some are saved. Second, Wesley finds a problem with antinomianism in them. They believed that faith alone is enough for a Christian without regard to the Christian life of following the revealed way God has given to us. Third, he found a type of quietism in them he could not accept. He finds in them a lack of emphasis upon works at all before becoming or after being justified. People are to wait in stillness for the Christian faith to come upon them rather than seeking God and using the means of grace as well as performing the good works which are the fruit of faith.

. . . I have read, and endeavoured to consider, all the books you have published in England, that I might inform myself whether, on farther consideration, you had retracted the errors which were advanced before. But it does by no means appear that you have retracted any of them: For, waiving the odd and affected phrases therein; the weak, mean, silly, childish expressions; the crude, confused, and indigested notions; the whims, unsupported either by Scripture or sound reason; yea, waiving those assertions which, though contrary to Scripture and matter of fact, are, however, of no importance; those three grand errors run through almost all those books, viz., *Universal Salvation, Antinomianism,* and a kind of new-reformed *Quietism.*[1]

Most of Wesley's writings in the Works which touch upon his war with the Moravians are found in Volume 10, which covers "An Extract from a Short View of the Difference between the Moravian Brethren, (so called,) and the Rev. Mr. John and Charles Wesley",[2] "A Dialogue between an Antinomianism and his Friend,[3] and "A Second Dialogue Between an Antinomian and His Friend."[4] Some information can be gleaned from Wesley's letters to the Rev. Mr. Church.[5] The other materials come from his Journal in Volume 1 entitled "To the Moravian Church," which contains most of the useful material of this war. [6]

Wesley begins his journal entries "To the Moravian Church" with praise for what he has learned from them and what they are doing right as far as he is concerned. In fact, he says his love for them kept him from writing before this time.[7] Wesley first met and was pleased with the Christianity he found among the Moravians in 1736 and he did not publish this until 1744, so he did hold back for some time. In 1739, his

---

1   Wesley, *Works*, 1:333

2   Wesley, *Works*, 10:201-4

3   Wesley, *Works*, 10:266-76

4   Wesley, *Works*, 10:276-84

5   Wesley, *Works*, 8:375-413

6   Wesley, *Works*, 1:243-335

7   Wesley, *Works*, 1:244

conflict with Philip Molther became pronounced and his conflicts with other Moravians heightened around this same period as well.

He compliments some of their doctrines such as God was in Christ reconciling the world to him, the grace of God is the cause and faith the condition of justification, the fruits of faith, and those who are born of God do not commit sin. He is stating his case here very carefully because if he fully spelled out what he believed in these areas they would already be in their theological war.

Wesley continues to compliment them because the Moravians, rather than rail out or be upset with how life has treated them or their position within society, accept their condition. They do not show the sins of the flesh or pride and they love one another. The outward sins of mankind are not found in them either. Likewise, their discipline among the members of the church and to its offices and those who are employed in serving the church is admirable.

He says he will go easy on them because he loves and respects them so much. He may say it and he certainly is not nearly as dramatic against them as he is against some others with whom he went to war, but he still manages to pull no punches when he gets down to their important differences as he perceives them.

It should be understood Wesley found differences among the Moravians. Some doctrinal problems of the war were in some individual or only some members of the church which are documented in his two letters to the Rev. Mr. Church. One example is the faith issue in which Wesley believes in degrees but Spangenberg does not.[8]

A. CHRISTIAN FAITH—COMPLETE OR GROWTH?

Wesley then gives examples of the problems he has with their theology by giving a historical summary using his Journals from November 1, 1739 to September 3, 1741. His problems began on November 1, 1739 in London when he met with one of the women who he left full of faith and now she believes she never had faith at all and because of this she was

---

[8]   Wesley, *Works*, 8:417

supposed to be quiet and cease from doing any good works until she had faith. These particular directions came from Molther.

He found out a few days later being quiet to the Moravians, at least to Molther and his followers, meant to abstain from all means of grace, especially the Lord's Supper and in fact what Wesley and others thought of as the means of grace really weren't such because grace was received only through Christ and belief in him. Molther had most of the Fetter-Lane Society believing they had no faith even though they had thought they had the faith before he arrived from Germany.

Wesley talked to Mr. August Gottlieb Spangenberg, who was a theologian, minister, and later became a Bishop of the Moravian Church, and he concluded:

> I agreed with all he said of the power of faith. I agreed, that "whosoever is" by faith "born of God doth not commit sin:" But I could not agree, either, that none has any faith, so long as he is liable to any doubt or fear; or, that till we have it, we ought to abstain from the Lord's Supper, or the other ordinances of God.[9]

Wesley then met with a woman who was in the Fetter-Lane Society who told him she had faith even though the followers of Molther tried to convince her she hadn't and she received her faith when she partook of the elements in the Lord's Supper. This experience related to him by the woman buttressed Wesley's belief in the necessity of the means of grace, and that we should use the means of grace because God may meet us in using them. Wesley concludes there are means of grace, the Lord's Supper is one of the means of grace, and we should use those means of grace even if we have not the faith but are seeking it.[10]

We are given a summary of the theologies in conflict or at war which is given after Wesley had a long conversation with Molther and which is found in the Journal on Monday, December 31, 1739. Molther believes there is only one kind of faith, or in other words, there are no degrees of faith for the Christian. You either have the complete Christian faith or

---

[9]   Wesley, *Works*, 1:247
[10] Wesley, *Works*, 1:248

you have no faith at all. This faith encompasses the assurance of faith and thus also being made a new being. This Christian has no doubts or fears. Justification is accompanied by the indwelling of the Holy Spirit. This is the first and only step of Christian faith.

> "1. There are no degrees of faith, and that no man has any degree of it, before all things in him are become new, before he has the full assurance of faith, the abiding witness of the Spirit, or the clear perception that Christ dwelleth in him.
>
> "2. Accordingly you believe, there is no justifying faith, or state of justification, short of this.
>
> "3. Therefore you believe, our brother Hutton, Edmonds, and others, had no justifying faith before they saw you.
>
> "4. And, in general, that that gift of God, which many received since Peter Bohler came into England, viz., 'a sure confidence of the love of God' to them, was not justifying faith.
>
> "5. And that the joy and love attending it were from animal spirits, from nature or imagination; not 'joy in the Holy Ghost,' and the real 'love of God shed abroad in their hearts.'"[11]

Wesley has several problems with this description of the Christian faith. He believes we may have a degree of faith before we receive the assurance of faith and even before we are made new. He is sure justifying faith comes before those gifts of God and he says many in the societies have received a faith which is full of joy and love, and this faith is truly from God, not from some animal spirits like Molther contends.

Wesley later describes more fully what this weak faith is for the Christian. If a Christian is worried he will not endure to the end or if this faith is mixed with doubt as to whether or not our sins are really forgiven, or again if there is still a lack of complete purification of the heart, Wesley says such a person has faith and he called it a weak faith. This weakness of faith is not just something Wesley dreamed up to fight about; because

---

[11]   Wesley, *Works*, 1:256-7

there is a scriptural basis for this thought. Wesley quotes from Paul, John and Jesus.

> "Yet that weak faith is faith appears, 1. From St. Paul, 'Him that is weak in faith, receive.' 2. From St. John, speaking of believers who were little children, as well as of young men and fathers. 3. From our Lord's own words, 'Why are ye fearful, O ye of little faith? O thou of little faith, wherefore didst thou doubt?—I have prayed for thee, (Peter,) that thy faith fail thee not.' Therefore he then had faith. Yet so weak was that faith that not only doubt and fear, but gross sin in the same night prevailed over him.
>
> "Nevertheless he was 'clean, by the word' Christ had 'spoken to him;' that is, justified; though it is plain he had not a clean heart.
>
> "Therefore, there are degrees in faith; and weak faith may yet be true faith."[12]

The Moravians, at least Spangenberg and Molther, appear to combine justification and sanctification calling the duo "faith," whereas Wesley sees a distinct separation of the two concepts though faith is necessary for both of them. For the Moravians the light switch is either on or off whereas for Wesley there is a dimmer switch which allows for growth in faith as one accepts more and more fully the graces of God.

For Wesley the single faith concept which combines justification and sanctification is a grave misreading of the scriptures, life, and good theology. One might or could use the term "salvation" to cover all the workings of God from the "first dawning of grace in the soul, till it is consummated in glory."[13]

Salvation normally, though, is combined with the concepts of justification and sanctification. Justification can be described as or mean being pardoned by God. All of our sins are forgiven and we have thus been accepted by God. This is an act not by man but by God wherein God paid the price for our sins through the death of Christ on the cross or in actuality the entire work of Jesus.

---

[12] Wesley, *Works*, 1:276
[13] Wesley, *Standard Sermons*, Vol. 2:445

Justification results in our receiving the peace which only God can give. Now we can rejoice, in hope, for our future of continued growth in love for God and man. At the same time we are justified the process of sanctification begins. It is not necessarily completed then because there is a lot of growth which must take place before one reaches full sanctification or Christian perfection. At the point where sanctification begins we are born again of God and there is a real and a relative change within us by God's grace.

> And at the same time that we are justified, yea, in that very moment, sanctification begins. In that instant we are born again, born from above, born of the Spirit; there is a *real* as well as a *relative* change. We are inwardly renewed by the power of God. We feel 'the love of God shed abroad in our heart by the Holy Ghost which is given unto us'; producing love to all mankind, and more especially to the children of God; expelling the love of the world, the love of pleasure, of peace, of honour, of money, together with pride, anger, self-will, and every other evil temper: in a word, changing the earthly, sensual, devilish mind, into 'the mind which was in Christ Jesus.'[14]

John himself had been confused in his early days but after his experiences before and after Aldersgate he discovered the differences between the two concepts of justification and sanctification and never wavered thereafter. Several distinctions between John's early definition of faith and his later are included in Sugden's introduction to the earlier sermon "Salvation by Faith" and his later one "The Scripture Way of Salvation."[15]

Often Christians, when they are first justified begin to believe they are cured of sin, says Wesley. Because they do not immediately feel sin and its effects as they did before, they assume it is gone. This belief is not true, because they very often feel sin start to arouse and move within them again. It is at this point they feel two natures within and find them at war with one another.

---

[14] Wesley, *Standard Sermons*, Vol. 2:446
[15] Wesley, *Standard Sermons*, Vol. 1:36

Though these Christians feel the power of God within, they love God and believe in Christ, they still sometimes feel pride, self-will, anger or unbelief.[16]

Since Wesley separated prevenient grace, justification, and sanctification and he also talked about the faith of a servant and that of a child of God, he could not accept the Moravian interpretation of faith as a single, complete faith, or no faith at all. The Christian faith, the experience of Christians with God's grace, and his reading of the scriptures would not allow him to agree with their definition.

B. CHRISTIAN FAITH—WAIT OR ACTIVELY SEEK IT?

The Moravian idea pushed especially by Molther was, if you did not have the complete Christian faith you were to pursue it by being "still." Further, the way to be still was to wait for Christ. Non Christians or incomplete Christians were to avoid what most of Christendom referred to as the means of grace, to refrain from attending church, avoid the Lord's Supper, do not fast, avoid private prayer, do not read the scriptures, and do not try to do anything which might be considered as good works which would be seen as an effort to save yourself. This concept seems strange to many of us who are Christians today. Though we could agree with the concept that our good works or any works for that matter, which result in our salvation, is a salvation by works; we cannot therefore agree with the Moravians that the way to seek salvation is to not seek it.

> "As to the way to faith, you believe,
> "That the way to attain it is, to wait for Christ, and be still; that is,
> "Not to use (what we term) the means of grace;
> "Not to go to church;
> "Not to communicate;
> "Not to fast;
> "Not to use so much private prayer;
> "Not to read the Scripture'

---

[16] Wesley, *Standard Sermons*, Vol. 2:447

"(Because you believe, these are not means of grace; that is, do not ordinarily convey God's grace to unbelievers; and,

"That it is impossible for a man to use them without trusting in them;)

"Not to do temporal good;

"Nor to attempt doing spiritual good.

"Because you believe, no fruit of the Spirit is given by those who have it not themselves;

"(And, that those who have not faith are utterly blind, and therefore unable to guide other souls.)[17]

This is quite a list of things Christians should avoid if they want to be a Christian but don't have the full assurance of Christ dwelling within them. Molther explained being still to Wesley concerning the means of grace in this way: if you have the full confidence of faith you do not need the means of grace and if you do not have the full confidence of faith you ought not to use them. In other words, those who are really Christian don't need the means of grace, because they are free from them and can use them or not, as they see fit. Those, however, who are not fully Christian, should not use them at all.

1. That there are *no degrees* in faith; that none has any faith who has ever any doubt or fear; and that none is justified till he has a clean heart, with the perpetual indwelling of Christ, and of the Holy Ghost; and, 2. That every one who has not this, ought, till he has it, to be *still*: That is, as he (Molther) explained it, not to use the ordinances, or means of grace, so called. [Parenthesis mine] He also expressly asserted, 1. That to those who have a clean heart, the ordinances are not matter of duty. They are not commanded to use them: They are free: They may use them, or they may not. 2. That those who have not a clean heart, ought not to use them; (particularly not to communicate;) because God neither commands nor designs they should; (commanding them to none, designing themselves for believers;) and because they are not means of grace; there being no such thing as means of grace, but Christ only.[18]

---

17   Wesley, *Works*, 1:257
18   Wesley, *Works*, 1:270

This is a very peculiar understanding of the means of grace, particularly for those in the Methodist and other traditions who are great believers in the sacraments.

The means of grace for Wesley are the outward signs, words or actions which have been ordained by God and appointed by him to be the ordinary channels through which God conveys to man three graces: prevenient, justifying, and sanctifying.

The means of grace Wesley is concerned with are prayer, reading the scriptures, and the Lord's Supper. So we have the definition of the means of grace and the listing of those means which the church through the ages has used and Wesley mentions. Now baptism is a means of grace also but it is not discussed by Wesley here, probably because most of those listening to his sermon would already have been baptized when they were infants.

> By 'means of grace,' I understand outward signs, words or actions, ordained of God, and appointed for this end, to be the ordinary channels whereby He might convey to men, preventing, justifying, or sanctifying grace.[19]

Naturally, one must be sure these means of grace are not viewed as magical or the belief if we go through the form or just perform them somehow magically God's grace will automatically be given to us. The means of grace are a means and must be accepted and used as such, they are not mechanical or magical, as though after so many repetitions or performances we will be given our just reward.

If these means are used separately from the Spirit of God they are meaningless. God is the one who works through the means of his grace and if any means be used apart from him, nothing is gained at all. There is no power or magic in the words which are spoken, in prayers, or in the words of scripture read, or in the bread and wine of the Lord's Supper. God alone works through these means and apart from him and his work they are really nothing.[20]

> Settle this in your heart, that the mere work done profits nothing. There is no power to save but in the Spirit of God,

---

[19]   Wesley, *Standard Sermons*, 1:242
[20]   Wesley, *Standard Sermons*, 1:243

no merit but in the blood of Christ. Consequently, even what God ordains conveys no grace to the soul if you do not trust in Him alone. On the other hand, he that does truly trust in Him cannot fall short of the grace of God, even though he were cut off from every outward ordinance or shut up in the center of the earth.

In using all means, seek God alone. In and through every outward thing, look only to the *power* of His Spirit, and the *merits* of His Son. Beware you do not get stuck in the *work* itself; if you do, it is all lost labor. Nothing short of God can satisfy your soul. Therefore, fix on Him in all, and though all, and above all. For all the power, and all the merit is of Him alone.

Remember also to use all means as *means*—as ordained, not for their own sake, but for the renewal of your soul in righteousness and true holiness. If, therefore, they actually tend to this, that is well; but if not, they are dung and dross.[21]

In fact God could choose to give Christians his grace through no means at all. He can so choose but he has given us certain means of grace which we are to use. Since God has given them to us to use we should obey Him and use them.

The means of grace by themselves really can do nothing to help us—all depends upon the sacrifice which Christ has made so we can be reconciled to God. We know, as believers in Christ, there is no merit in our works, even in our using the means of grace. All is of Christ and what is not of Christ is nothing.

One hymn written during and about this controversy shows the power of the Wesleyan understanding of God's work (grace) and our response.

Author of faith, to thee I cry,
To thee, who wouldst not have me die,
But know the truth, and live;
Open mine eyes to see thy face,
Work in my heart the saving grace,
The life eternal give.

---

[21]   Wesley, *How To Pray*, 16

Shut up in unbelief I groan,
And blindly serve a god unknown,
Till thou the veil remove;
The gift unspeakable impart,
And write thy name upon my heart,
And manifest thy love.

I know the work is only thine,
The gift of faith is all divine;
But if on thee we call,
Thou wilt the benefit bestow,
And give us hearts to feel and know
That thou hast died for all.

Thou bidd'st us knock and enter in,
Come unto thee, and rest from sin,
The blessing seek and find:
Thou bidd'st us ask thy grace, and have:
Thou canst, thou wouldst, this moment save
Both me and all mankind.

Be it according to thy word!
Now let me find my pardoning Lord:
Let what I ask be given;
The bar of unbelief remove,
Open the door of faith and love,
And take me into heaven![22]

Unfortunately Wesley believes there are many who use the means of grace incorrectly and so are not helped by using them. Some may believe they are Christians already because they perform certain acts; yet they have not received Christ into their hearts and they do not shed abroad the love of God which is in their hearts. Some believe if they use the means of grace, God's grace will be given to them at some point merely because they use them. No, the grace we receive through using the means of grace given by God is not due to anything we might do, rather it is by the free grace given to us by the God who performed mighty works through His Son, Jesus the Christ.

---

[22]   Wesley, *Wesley's Hymns*, #118

Still someone may say they know salvation comes from God, but how can I go about receiving it? Such an important question must be answered for us somewhere—God would not leave us without some instruction. The instruction is found in the scriptures. We are to use the means of grace which God has given us, and not disregard them.

> According to this, according to the decision of holy writ, all who desire the grace of God are to wait for it in the means which He hath ordained: in using, not in laying them aside.[23]

As far as prayer is concerned Wesley says we are directed by Jesus to pray in the Sermon on the Mount when he says to the multitude "So I say to you, Ask, and it will be given you; search, and you will find; knock and the door will be opened for you. For everyone who asks receives, and everyone who searches finds, and for everyone who knocks, the door will be opened." (NRSV Lk. 11:9-10) Wesley comments that the person referred to in this case was one who had not received the Holy Spirit and yet Jesus tells this person to ask, search, and knock and in this way they will receive the Holy Spirit.

Another parable which relates to praying as a means of grace concerns a judge and a widow who has little standing in the court and certainly nothing to give, nevertheless receives grace from the judge because she is persistent. In like manner such persistence by a Christian will surely result in God's grace being given.

Again, Jesus admonishes us to pray in secret rather than before people wherein we receive the honors and plaudits from others rather than God. Wesley says from these and many other scriptures he believes if we want to receive the grace of God rather than ceasing to pray we are to continue praying.

So if prayer definitely is a means of grace and we are to use it, what about reading scripture? Wesley quotes Jesus "You search the scriptures because you think that in them you have eternal life; and it is they that testify on my behalf."(John 5:39 NRSV) So Jesus directed them to read the scriptures. Wesley thinks of reading the scriptures as including reading, meditating, and hearing the scriptures.

---

23   Wesley, *Standard Sermons,* 1:245

It is probable, indeed, in some of those who had 'received the word with all readiness of mind,' 'faith came,' as the same Apostle speaks, 'by hearing,' and was only confirmed by reading the Scriptures: but it was observed above, that, under the general term of searching the Scriptures, both hearing, reading, and meditating are contained.[24]

He also illustrates this point by discussing Paul's letter to Timothy in which Paul says the people of Berea have read the scriptures about what Paul has been preaching concerning Jesus and in so doing many of them believed.

Not only does Wesley find the Old Testament profitable for man to read, because naturally Paul is talking about the Old Testament, he finds it important for us to read the New Testament as well.[25] Wesley tells us we are to pray and to read the scriptures, but what about the Lord's Supper, is it one of the means of grace we should also use?

The first thing to be said is Christ himself tells us to partake of the Supper.[26] We are to partake in remembrance of him until he comes again. Wesley finds a command for us to partake in these verses. Jesus' command is given to all who already are Christian believers or who are sorry for their sins. The Lord's Supper is a normal way, or means of finding the grace of God.

> And that this is also an ordinary, stated means of receiving the grace of God, is evident from those words of the Apostle which occur in the preceding chapter: 'The cup of blessing which we bless, is it not the communion,' or *communication*, 'of the blood of Christ? The bread which we break, is it not the communion of the body of Christ?' . . . Is not the eating of that bread, and the drinking of that cup, the outward, visible means whereby God conveys into our souls all that spiritual grace, that righteousness, and peace, and joy in the Holy Ghost, which were purchased by the body of Christ once broken, and the blood of Christ once shed for us? Let all, therefore, who

---

[24] Wesley, *Standard Sermons*, 1:249
[25] Wesley, *Standard Sermons*, 1:250-1
[26] Wesley, *Standard Sermons*, 1:252

truly desire the grace of God, eat of that bread, and drink of that cup.[27]

Wesley answers some of the common objections which a few of the Moravians raise against the use of the means of grace. The first objection they have is we are not to use the means of grace without trusting in those means. There is no place in the scriptures where Wesley can find such an objection. Certainly Jesus did not know of such a thing or he would have told us.

If one would tell us in this regard to just try going without using these means for awhile to see if we trust them, Wesley answers he can't go without them because to do so is to disobey God.

The second objection is seeking after God and his grace through the means of grace is nothing more than seeking salvation by works. Wesley points to St. Paul's discussion where he talks about seeking salvation by works and says he is either referring to following the ritual works of the Mosaic law or seeking salvation on the basis of our own works and the merit supposedly gained thereby. Wesley says neither of these have anything to do with what are talking about.

> I do expect that He will fulfill His word, that He will meet and bless me in this way. Yet not for the sake of any works which I have done, nor for the merit of my righteousness: but merely through the merits, and sufferings, and love of His Son, in whom He is always well pleased.[28]

The third objection of the Moravians is it is Christ alone who is the means of grace. Wesley says this objection is meaningless because all agree. By using any of the means of grace we understand that in order for them to be effective God must work through them.

The fourth objection is the scripture itself tells us to wait upon salvation. Yes, we are to wait on God for salvation but how are we to wait? God has given us a way to wait and we are to use the means of grace as we wait. Wesley answers the question so completely when he says:

---

27 Wesley, *Standard Sermons*, 1:252-3
28 Wesley, *Standard Sermons*, 1:254

If you say, "Believe, and you will be saved!" they answer, "True, but how shall I believe?" You reply, "Wait upon God."

"Well, but how am I to wait? Using the means of grace, or not? Am I to wait for the grace of God, which brings salvation by using the means of grace, or by laying them aside?"

It cannot be conceived that the Word of God should give no direction in so important a point; or that the Son of God, who came down from heaven for us and for our salvation, should have left us without direction with regard to a question in which our salvation is so nearly concerned. And, in fact, He has *not* left us undirected; He has shown us the way in which we should go. We have only to consult the Word of God. Inquire what is written there. If we simply abide by that, no possible doubt can remain.

According to holy scripture, all who desire the grace of God are to wait for it in the means which He has ordained—*in using, not in laying aside*, prayer; hearing, reading, and meditating on the scriptures; and partaking of the Lord's Supper.[29]

The fifth has to do with standing "still" and waiting for God to act and refers to when the children of Israel were leaving Egypt and the Egyptians were after them. Moses told them to stand still and see God's salvation and God then told Moses to tell the Israelites to go forward. So one supposes God has told the Israelites they are to stay still while moving forward. "This is the *salvation of God*, which they *stood still* to see, by *marching forward* with all their might!"[30]

The way in which we use the means is important also. We are to remember God is even greater than the means of Grace. God can convey his grace though any means he desires. God is not limited in giving his grace.

Before you use any means of grace you should be aware the performance of the means of grace is meaningless apart from God working in and through them. The means are not what is important. Rather, it is God's grace working through them. The means are not magic; they have no power

---

29   Wesley, *How to Pray*, p. 37

30   Wesley, *Standard Sermons*, 1:255

in themselves. It is the fact God works through them which is the important point. This thought is said so well in the Hymns for Methodists.

> The cup of blessing, bless'd by thee,
> Let it thy blood impart;
> The bread thy mystic body be,
> And cheer each languid heart.
> The grace which sure salvation brings
> Let us herewith receive;
> Satiate the hungry with good things,
> The hidden manna give.
>
> The living bread, sent down from heaven,
> In us vouchsafe to be:
> Thy flesh for all the world is given,
> And all may live by thee.
> Now, Lord, on us thy flesh bestow,
> And let us drink thy blood,
> Till all our souls are fill'd below
> With all the life of God. [31]

There is also no power in the means of grace apart from God's work for our salvation through Christ. The means are a way of seeking God; this is their purpose and their power. Upon using any means of grace remember the significant fact is not what you have done but what you have received.

> If God was there, if His love flowed into your heart, you have forgot, as it were, the outward work. You see, you know, you feel, God is all in all. Be abased. Sink down before Him. Give Him all the praise. 'Let God in all things be glorified through Christ Jesus.' Let all your bones cry out,
> 'My song shall be always of the lovingkindness of the Lord: with my mouth will I ever be telling of Thy truth from one generation to another!'[32]

---

[31]   Wesley, *Wesley's Hymns*, #549, vss. 3,4
[32]   Wesley, *Standard Sermons*, 1:260

So ends the discussion of the means of grace and the correct use of the means of grace between the Moravians and the Wesleyans. The means of grace are to be used by all Christians and by all who are seeking to become Christians. One should seek God until we are found by God, using all of the means possible which God has given us. Stillness or quietism is not to be followed by those who follow Wesley for we are activists, we seek, and we knock so we can receive God's grace.

Charles Wesley pretty well sums up the thinking of the Methodists in one of his poems on the Lord's Supper which he wrote about the time of the stillness controversy and in reply to those who believed in stillness.

> The word pronounced, the Gospel-word,
> The crowd with various hearts received:
> In many a soul the Saviour stirr'd,
> Three thousand yielded, and believed.
>
> These by the apostles' counsels led,
> With them in mighty prayer combined,
> Broke the commemorative bread,
> Nor from the fellowship declined.
>
> God from above, with ready grace
> And deeds of wonder, guards His flock;
> Trembles the world before their face,
> By Jesus crush'd their Conquering Rock.
>
> The happy band whom Christ redeems,
> One only will, one judgment know:
> None of this contentious earth esteems,
> Distinctions or delights below . . . [33]

C. CLOSING COMMENTS

For all their emphasis upon belief and belief is the only thing necessary for salvation, the Moravians have a peculiar way of expressing it. Some of their presentations would lead to everyone being saved in the final analysis.

---

[33] Tyson, John, *Assist Me to Proclaim*, 94

They believe and teach,—

"1. That Christ has done all which was necessary for the salvation of all mankind.

"2. That, consequently, we are to do nothing, as necessary to salvation, but simply to believe in him.

"3. That there is but one duty now, but one command, viz., to believe in Christ.

"4. That Christ has taken away all other commands and duties, having wholly 'abolished the law;' that a believer is therefore 'free from the law,' is not obliged thereby to do or omit anything; it being inconsistent with his liberty to do anything as commanded.[34]

It would not appear necessary to believe all men are saved from the position of the Moravians in which is belief is enough. However, if you are going to posit universal salvation, starting in this way is as good as any in order to get there.

There is not a lot of time or effort by Wesley in discussing this issue. It does come up in the discussions between "An Antinomian and His Friend" and "A Second Dialogue between an Antinomian and his Friend."[35]

The antinomian here says the total work of salvation was accomplished or performed by Jesus on the cross. The antinomian pushes further to say by the blood of Christ our sins totally went away.[36] In the fullest statement the antinomian says:

. . . Why, did not Christ, "when he was upon the cross, take away, put an end to, blot out, and utterly destroy, all our sins for ever?" . . .

I mean, He did then "heal, take away, put an end to, and utterly destroy, all our sins."[37]

The response of Wesley throughout is Christ died on the cross and in so doing he paid the price for our sins. If we truly believe in him and if we endure to the end we will be saved everlastingly.

---

[34] Wesley, *Works*, 10:201-2

[35] Wesley, *Works*, 10:266-84

[36] Wesley, *Works*, 10:266

[37] Wesley, *Works*, 10:267

After writing and separating his Journal from November 1, 1739 to September 3, 1741, which he prepared as an answer to the Moravian Church and the problems he had with them, John summarized the three main problems he had with them.

> Three things, above all, permit *me*, even *me*, to press upon you, with all the earnestness of love. First, With regard to your doctrine, that ye purge out from among you the leaven of Antinomianism, wherewith you are so deeply infected, and no longer "make void the Law through faith." Secondly, With regard to your discipline, that ye "call no man Rabbi, Master," Lord of your faith, "upon earth." Subordination, I know, is needful; and I can show you such a subordination, as in fact answers all Christian purposes, and is yet as widely distant from that among *you*, as the heavens are from the earth. Thirdly, With regard to your practice, that ye renounce all craft, cunning, subtlety, dissimulation; wisdom, falsely so called; that ye put away all disguise, all guile out of your moth; that in all "simplicity and godly sincerity" ye "have your conversation in this world;" that ye use "great plainness of speech" to all, whatever ye suffer thereby; seeking only, "by manifestation of the truth," to "commend" yourselves "to every man's conscience in the sight of God."[38]

Wesley talked of other things but these are the main ones other than the Christian life, sanctification, or Christian perfection. In the area of Christian living or sanctification they had significant differences but this doctrine is best covered apart from the Moravians since the war of Christian perfection involved more than the Moravians.

---

[38] Wesley, *Works*, 1:335

4

JOHN WESLEY AND THE CHURCH OF ENGLAND

Another theological battle or war is engaged by Wesley pretty much throughout his career. This is the theological battle with the Church of England about what the "Church" really meant and by inference how the Methodists fit in that definition and with the Church of England. Several Bishops and a multitude of the clergy were against Wesley in this battle.

Wesley faces many accusations across the years in regards to his relationship with the Church of England as well as many other things. He is described as a papist (Roman Catholic) in disguise, an enthusiast, an antinomian, as well as other things. None of these descriptions put forward by his enemies are correct. The accusations flew at him throughout his ministry and he tried to combat them many times. I'm sure he became very tired of having to cover the same material over and over. His critics seem not to have read his last several efforts to explain himself because they apparently think they have discovered a "new" criticism of Wesley and are ardent in their pursuit of some of the same issues discussed and handled many times before.

Wesley defends himself in "An Earnest Appeal to Men of Reason and Religion,"[1] "A Farther Appeal to Men of Reason and Religion",[2] "A Plain Account of the People Called Methodists",[3] "The Character of a

---

[1]   Wesley, *Works*, 8:3-45
[2]   Wesley, *Works*, 8:46-247
[3]   Wesley, *Works*, 8:248-68

Methodist",[4] and a letter to the Rev. Mr. Church,[5] "The Principles of a Methodist Further Explained,"[6] and "A Letter to the Right Rev. The Lord Bishop of London."[7]

Some of his outlandish practices which helped fuel this fight were that he had the audacity to sing hymns, preach without a manuscript, give extemporary prayer, and engage in outdoor preaching. All of these were practices which most Anglican priests at the time would carefully avoid. Today most ministers would not even raise a theological eyebrow in doing all of these except perhaps field preaching, and even field preaching might be all right at least on Easter Sunday morning or in camping with youth or adults.

Though Wesley remained an Anglican priest until the day he died, he did prepare the Methodists to become a church in their own right after being denied his first choice, which was to make the Methodists into a leavening element within the Church of England which would continue long after his death. In addition, any leaning towards separation brought him into conflict with his brother who likewise was an Anglican priest and wanted to remain such and wanted the Methodists to remain within the Church of England.

Though an occasional Bishop for a time might support Wesley's endeavors, he seldom was able to get many at one time or one for any length of time to support him.

A. THE BISHOPS

Early in their ministry John and Charles were lucky because they knew both the Bishop of London and the Archbishop of Canterbury. After all, Dr. John Potter of Canterbury had been a Fellow of Lincoln College and he had ordained both John and Charles as deacons and John as a priest. Potter did think John and Charles had a chance of leavening the Church of England; at least he thought so during the early years of the Wesley's work.

---

4   Wesley, *Works*, 8:339-47

5   Wesley, *Works*, 8:375-481

6   Wesley, *Works*, 8:413-413

7   Wesley, *Works*, 8:481-95

At first the Bishop of London, Edmund Gibson, seemed to understand their work. He ordained Charles as a priest so there was a personal tie which may have indeed helped them for awhile.

The brothers had to appear before Gibson on October 20, 1738 in order to answer charges against them concerning doctrine and discipline. The sessions with him during 1738 seemed to go pretty well but they did receive some warnings to watch out for antinomianism. The brothers were resolved to work within the Church of England, to defend its doctrines as they understood them, and to create societies in order to revitalize the Church of England.

Societies were not new in London. There were societies for various activities, even some of the religious variety, so the concept of a society dedicated to religion was not entirely foreign to folks in 18th century England. However, it was not long before the situation and the understanding between the Wesley's and the Church of England began to change.

One of the hymns portrays the closeness of one to another and even reflects the supervision which the societies, bands, and classes allow.

> Jesu, we look to thee,
> Thy promised presence claim!
> Thou in the midst of us shalt be,
> Assembled in thy name.
> Thy name salvation is,
> Which here we come to prove;
> Thy name is life, and health, and peace,
> And everlasting love.

> Not in the name of pride
> Or selfishness we meet;
> From nature's paths we turn aside,
> And worldly thoughts forget.
> We meet, the grace to take
> Which thou hast freely given;
> We meet on earth for thy dear sake,
> That we may meet in heaven.

> Present we know thou art;
> But O thyself reveal!

Now, Lord, let every bounding heart
The mighty comfort feel!
O may thy quick'ning voice
The death of sin remove;
And bid our inmost souls rejoice
In hope of perfect love![8]

The Wesley's did not want to preach in the parish of another priest without permission if it could first be obtained. George Whitfield began field preaching, which was soon to be followed by the Wesley's. They first sought the use of local churches, but if they were turned down by the local church or the church was unable to accommodate the crowd, they then spoke in the open.

John was a fellow of Oxford and as such did not have a parish to which he was located or tied to a particular church location like many other priests, and neither was Charles. This allowed them to preach anywhere and not be in the wrong. At least they were not wrong according to church law but some, if not many, of the clergy did not like it.

The Anglican priests of the day were accustomed to preach from written manuscripts and to exclusively pray the prayers found in the Book of Common Prayer. John began deviating from this common and accepted practice as far back as his American experience. He preached on shipboard without a manuscript and began extemporary prayers soon after his return to England. He then used the written prayers or extemporary prayers as he thought best suited the occasion. These two practices by the brother's Wesley set them apart from the other Anglican priests. This made them and their practices different and marked them as being not like the rest of the regular clergy.

These two differences followed by field preaching or preaching outdoors, further strained the brother's relationship with the Anglican Church. Wesley had reasons for this move even though it was begun apparently somewhat hesitantly. It is generally accepted Whitfield's preaching was more spectacular than Wesley's and Wesley was less cantankerous in his publications against the authorities. Because of this practice John was able

---

[8]   Wesley, *Wesley's Hymns*, #485

to sidestep many of the attacks which Whitfield received. However, at times the attacks were such they were all tarred with the same brush.

In order to totally understand the reaction of the Anglican Church, it's leaders, and priests, one must study the history of the time. We do not have the time, talent, nor space for such a study. Such a study is outside the parameters of our work and would take much more space than is allotted to this book.

Needless to say, as things progressed the Wesley's were not welcomed in hardly any Anglican churches and their field preaching was the only recourse for them other than a few places they eventually owned and were setup for the Methodists, such as the Fetter-Lane Society and later the Foundry.

> Be pleased to observe: (1.) That I was for bidden, as by a general consent, to preach in any church, (though not by any judicial sentence,) "for preaching such doctrine." This was the open, avowed cause; there was at that time no other, either real or pretended, except that the people crowded so. (2.) That I had no desire or design to preach in the open air, till after this prohibition. (3.) That when I did, as it was no matter of choice, so neither of premeditation. There was no scheme at all previously formed, which was to be supported thereby; nor had I any other end in view than this,—to save as many souls as I could. (4.) Field-preaching was therefore a sudden expedient, a thing submitted to, rather than chosen; and therefore submitted to, because I thought preaching even thus, better than not preaching at all: First, in regard to my own soul, because, "a dispensation of the gospel being committed to me," I did not dare "not to preach the gospel:" Secondly, in regard to the souls of others, whom I everywhere saw "seeking death in the error of their life."[9]

The changes John made from the normal Church of his lifetime seemed often to arise as a coming together of development of his thought and the necessities of the time for him to continue his unique ministry. You could call it a unique coming together of his theology and his new practice in the

---

[9]   Wesley, *Works*, 8:112-13

Methodist societies. Surely the hand of God was leading Wesley to prepare him for the necessities required for the continuation of the societies.

John did not have a "Master Plan" from the start of how to go about forming a church called the Methodist Church. Through events he deemed necessary and logical, he was moved gradually in this direction. Many incremental steps were required to get him to a particular position. Each step in itself was not always very much by itself, but the accumulation of them eventually became so large even Wesley could not stop the logical progression.

At the very least, the Wesley's and the Methodist societies were considered as unusual and enthusiasts. Enthusiasm is a word which seems to be a trash bin for everything somebody does not like, so it is useful in ascribing it to the Wesley's by their adversaries, even though the user of the term might not know what is really meant by the word.

Even when they tried to preach in the Anglican pulpits first they were soon forced out of them and into field preaching. Apparently some of those who were not happy with the Wesley's eventually found something in the canon's which allowed them not to accept preachers who did not have a handwritten license from the Bishop to preach in a specific parish. Since the Wesley's did not have such a license and were highly unlikely to get one, they were forced to continue their field preaching if they were to continue the work they believed they were called of God to perform.

First Wesley had to fight with the Church of England concerning his work which he believed was in support of the Church rather than against it. His "An Earnest Appeal to Men of Reason and Religion" takes care to point out this definition of a church.

> This being promised, I ask, How do we undermine or destroy
> the Church—the provincial, visible Church of England? The
> article mentions three things as essential to a visible Church.
> First: Living faith; without which, indeed there can be no
> Church at all, neither visible nor invisible. Secondly: Preaching,
> and consequently hearing, the pure word of God, else that faith
> would languish and die. And, Thirdly: a due administration of
> the sacraments,—the ordinary means whereby God increaseth

> faith. Now come close to the question: In which of these points
> do we undermine or destroy the Church?[10]

If, indeed, the Church is composed of these three things then there is no way at this point in time the Anglican Church can realistically charge Wesley with undermining or separating from the Church. At this point the so called Methodists were encouraged to attend the Church of England and to partake of the sacraments there. The sacraments could only be given by a priest and Wesley had precious few who would help him so the Methodists had to rely on ministers of the Church of England to provide their followers with the sacrament of the Lord's Supper.

As far as leaving the Church, Wesley points out the Methodists have not left the Church. In fact, many of the Methodists were in no church or were in churches other than the Church of England before they became Methodists. Also, society members were all encouraged to attend the Church of England and to receive their sacraments there.

Wesley came to believe the classes and bands were an important part of the leavening process of the Church which the Church of England was by and large missing. There is a closeness and personal relationship available and necessary in the bands and classes of the Methodists which the Church of England did not have.

Bringing into membership those who had "a desire to flee from the wrath to come, to be saved from their sins," Wesley soon sees more is required in order for them to really become a leaven in the Church of England.

So often in the early days Wesley observes those who were brought into the societies and who were excited about Christ soon lose their enthusiasm and their way, gradually drifting apart. In a few months they are back where they were before responding to the preaching of the word. Obviously, something additional is needed in order to help them to continue in the societies and to grow in the Christian life.

In his study of the early church Wesley thought he found the answer for retaining those in how the church handled new people who came into their fellowship. Wesley's answer, based on the early church and modernized for his day, is the societies followed by the creation of classes

---

10   Wesley, *Works*, 8:31

and bands. These groups gave him the small group experience of these who were 'fleeing from the wrath to come," and provided the way in which these who gathered together could help one another in their mutual journey.

As good as this may sound to us today, there were plenty who said this grouping together of people into societies, bands, and classes was somehow making a schism with the Church of England. Wesley answers this question by defining schism.

> I ask once more, What do you mean by schism? "Schism! Schism! why, it is separating from the Church." Ay, so it is. And yet every separating from the Church to which we once belonged is not schism; else you will make all the English to be schismatics, by separating from the Church of Rome. "But we had just cause." So doubtless we had; whereas schism is a causeless separation from the Church of Christ. So far so good. But you have many steps to take before you can make good that conclusion, that a separation from a particular national Church, such as the Church of England is, whether with sufficient cause or without, comes under the scriptural notion of schism.
>
> However, taking this for granted, will you aver in cool blood, that all who die in such a separation, that is, every one who dies a Quaker, a Baptist, an Independent, or a Presbyterian, is as infallibly damned as if he died in the act of murder or adultery? Surely you start at the thought! It makes even nature recoil. How can you reconcile it to the love that "Hopeth all things?"[11]

Yes, some who came to the societies had attended the Church of England but Wesley was still not dividing Christians from Christians because he said those people who joined the Methodists were not really Christians. In fact he said most were heathens. Wesley says they were not Christians even when they were in the Church of England. Neither was there true fellowship between the Methodists and those who remained within the Church of England.

---

[11] Wesley, *Works*, 8:235-6

"We introduce Christian fellowship where it was utterly destroyed. And the fruits of it have been peace, joy, love, and zeal for every good word and work."[12]

The societies are considered by some to be a division of Methodists from the Church of England. Wesley attacks this idea by returning to the definition of a Church and then pointing out by this definition the societies are not dividing but are more aimed towards uniting the Church

> *Leave the Church!* What can you mean? Do we leave so much as the Church walls? Your own eyes tell you we do not. Do we leave the ordinances of the Church? You daily see and know the contrary. Do we leave the fundamental doctrine of the Church, namely, salvation by faith? It is our constant theme, in public, in private, in writing, in conversation. Do we leave the practice of the Church, the standard whereof are the ten commandments? which are so essentially in-wrought in her constitution, (as little as you may apprehend it,) that whosoever breaks some of the least of these is no member of the Church of England. I believe you do not care to put the cause on this issue. Neither do you mean this by leaving the Church. In truth, I cannot conceive what you mean. I doubt you cannot conceive yourself. You have retailed a sentence from somebody else, which you no more understand than he . . . Nearly related to this is that other objection, that we divide the Church. Remember, the Church is the faithful people, or true believers. Now, how do we divide these? "Why, by our societies." Very good. Now the case is plain. "We divide them," you say, "by uniting them together." Truly, a very uncommon way of dividing.[13]

This apparently was the main belief or problem which the Church of England had with the Methodists at this time and Wesley answers the theological problem of the church in this way.

---

[12] Wesley, *Works*, 8:252
[13] Wesley, *Works*, 8:35-36

B. CHURCHMANSHIP

One of the primary areas of doctrine affecting his relationship with the Church of England has to do with Wesley's concept of the Church. Indeed many find two concepts of the Church which Wesley responds to in his ministry.

The first concept or definition of the Church is it is a historic institution which is related to the apostolic church by a succession of bishops and customs or ways in which the priest and people should act. Within this institution the priests were the ones who expounded and interpreted the Scriptures and who administered the sacraments. All of the institution was geared to preserve the traditions which were handed down for each generation of believers. This concept defined the church as an ancient institution to be preserved and which had traditions which were important to maintain within that institution.

The second concept or definition of the Church is a fellowship of believers who shared two main experiences. The first experience is an experience of God's living and personal presence and the second is a desire to find ways to bring or introduce others into the same experience. Various methods of evangelism and worship which seemed to work for those who were being led by the spirit of God were used. This concept defined the Church as a faithful few or remnant, who have a living relationship with God and each other.

John grew up in a household which was very aware of the first definition. His education and training followed this definition also. He became familiar with the second definition from a variety of sources such as by his parents, then the Moravians, and finally by some of his studies. John was forever the student. His reading was extraordinarily wide and deep.

The definition of the Church as a fellowship of believers is to be found in action and real life by the Moravians. This new way of personal experience of God had to be tested by scripture, reason, and experience by him in order for him to be certain. He also continued to use prayer and the sacraments.

> This once experienced (a personal assurance of salvation by faith in Jesus Christ as the 'one thing needful') all else took on a supporting rather than a determining significance, and he *knew* by the immediate authorization of the Holy Spirit that at that moment he was right with God, and that his time and talents *must all be devoted* to introducing others to this same rich experience. [Parenthesis mine] This he wished to do within the ordered ways of the Church of England, but if that proved impossible he would be ready to accept any method that was not contrary to the Scriptures, reason, and the voice of God within, and would be ready also to suffer whatever ridicule, censure, or persecution, official or non-official, which this personal following of Providence, might generate.[14]

Even though he was venturing into the second definition of the Church he, nonetheless, checked each step of this process by the ancient fathers, reason, and scriptures as well as prayer, to make sure he was not making a misstep.

By this time Wesley had been aware of and influenced by a wide and diverse emphasis within Christianity as well as the Spanish-speaking Jews. Consider his close relationship with the Moravians, the Presbyterians in Scotland, as well as some works by Richard Baxter. Though not complete, he kept moving towards a more complex theology as well as a more ecumenical appreciation of the Christian faith. He hesitatingly inched ever towards the second definition of the Church.

In reality, for Wesley, the two definitions of the Church are not "either, or." For him the definition was "both."

An evidence of his changing views of the Church started right at the beginning of his ministry after he returns from America he then agrees to meet with a group in London and he begins the process of becoming their spiritual leader. This group grew and became a society which is a name used at the time for different kinds of groups which gathered together by common interest. The difference here is this society was religious and owed their continuance to Wesley and not to any Church. It was here in London, they were first called a "United Society."

---

[14]   Baker, *John Wesley and the Church of England*, 139

After implementing his bands and classes Wesley appointed lay leaders who became the spiritual leaders of these smaller groups. The lay leaders were changed from time to time and not allowed to be permanent or even semi-permanent. Though they did not have services at the same time as the Anglican Church they did have services. General Rules were published and handed out to all who entered. At this point he did not allow lay people to preach.

The logical breakdown of Baker's into two definitions of the Church is good and provides us with some interesting information, but I personally prefer the triple definition of the Church which Wesley held and which is found in the work of Colin Williams.[15]

In his "Earnest Appeal" Wesley gives us his definition of the Church which we have quoted earlier (#10, p. 109-10). The three elements for a church are: a living faith, preaching the pure word of God, and the due administration of the sacraments.

Wesley says according to the Church of England homilies faith is defined as "a sure trust and confidence in God that through the merits of Christ my sins are forgiven, and I reconciled to the favor of God."

It is instructive to find these three things are required for the existence of the Church. Even though we may agree on these three, we find ourselves sometimes far apart due to the emphasis we place on each of them. For instance, if we place the emphasis heavier upon the due administration of the sacrament and go further to make the definition include the due administration in terms of an unbroken apostolic succession, we find ourselves with the same emphasis as the Roman Catholic Church.

If, on the other hand, we place our emphasis upon the second part of the definition which is preaching the word of God and hearing that word, we will find ourselves in the Protestant camp following the reformers.

Further, if we place our emphasis upon the first point, living faith, we find ourselves in the Free Church or holiness groups. To emphasize one of these three does not dismiss out of hand the other two, it just emphasizes one portion of the definition stronger than the others.

Wesley believes in order to be the church these three must be kept together, regardless of how difficult and impossible this may be to imagine.

---

15   Williams, *John Wesley's Theology Today*, 142

Another way of putting it is the holiness of the church is in the life of the church which expresses it, and the holiness of the church is found in its sacrament, and the holiness of the church is to be found in the Protestant emphasis of justification by faith and the life which results from this relationship.

> Wesley's claim is that unless the objective holiness, in terms of the given presence of Christ in the Word and sacraments, brings forth the subjective holiness of a living response in believers, the Church is not truly the Church. The given holiness in sacramental life and the objective holiness of the Word through preaching, should result in the subjective holiness through the faith relationship that is evoked. All three of these emphases Wesley believed to be essential to the being and the mission of the Church.[16]

The question at this point is "O.K. John, we get it. All three definitions of the Church are to be kept together but how in the world can you keep all of them together here in this world?" Wesley seems to answer this question by his organization of societies within the Church of England. The societies were constructed to be a leaven for the Church of England and they certainly were a leaven, even though they were not often recognized or appreciated by others, especially the bishops and priests, as such. The members of the societies received the word from John and his lay preachers and they disciplined themselves to be holy and thus perform their function as leaven within the Church of England.

Wesley was a great believer in the Protestant emphasis upon the preaching of the Word. However, even as strong as his emphasis is upon preaching the Word, he recognizes this is, or may be an impossible thing to ask. He says the definition in article 19 states the church is where ". . . the pure word of God is preached . . ."[17] This poses a problem for Wesley because he believes it is a bit much to expect, especially if you go to the next step and say it excludes any congregation in which the "pure word of God" is not preached.

---

16 Williams, *John Wesley's Theology Today*, 149
17 Wesley, *Works*, 6:397

> I dare not exclude from the Church catholic all those congregations in which any unscriptural doctrines, which cannot be affirmed to be the "pure word of God," are sometimes, yea, frequently preached; neither all those congregations, in which the sacraments are not "duly administered." Certainly if these things are so, the Church of Rome is not so much as a part of the catholic Church; seeing therein neither is "the pure word of God" preached, nor the sacraments "duly administered." Whoever they are that have "one Spirit, one hope, one Lord, one faith, one God and Father of all," I can easily bear with their holding wrong opinions, yea, and superstitious modes of worship: Nor would I, on these accounts, scruple still to include them within the pale of the catholic Church; neither would I have any objection to receive them, if they desired it, as members of the Church of England.[18]

Wesley also looked at the Church as a holy catholic or universal church and defined it in a series of statements about such a Church. This Church would be of one Spirit. All members of this Church would severally and individually respond to the Spirit and the Spirit would be found in each of them. This Spirit he says can be either the Holy Spirit or the spiritual gifts which these members receive.

Not only are these members of one Spirit but they also have "one hope." The hope which he is talking about is the hope of immortality. For them their physical death is not the end; all is not lost because we live in the hope of resurrection.

One Spirit, one hope and "one Lord." This Lord is their king and he rules over them. This Lord rules over his kingdom. They live to fulfill his commandments and open their lives to ever receive more of him.

Further, these people have "one faith." This faith is the gift of God which we can only accept from him because if we have faith we did not deserve or earn it. This faith is graciously given to us by God. Wesley tells us this faith is more than the faith of a heathen and also more than the faith of a devil. The heathen may believe in a God and the devil knows the scriptures are true. The faith Wesley speaks about is the faith which leads one to say "My Lord, and my God." Such faith allows us to testify

---

[18] Wesley, *Works*, 6:397

with Paul that the Son of God who died for me now lives and reigns within me.

The members of this church have "one baptism." This baptism is the outward sign of all the graces God continues to give to his Church.

Finally, this one true Church, this catholic or universal church has one God and Father of us all. In this Church we find those who have been adopted by God and as such we can address him as Father.

After all of this Wesley summarizes by saying:

> There, then, is a clear unexceptionable answer to that question, "What is the Church?" The catholic or universal Church is, all the persons in the universe whom God hath so called out of the world as to entitle them to the preceding character; as to be "one body," united by, "one Spirit;" having "one faith, one hope, one baptism; one God and Father of all, who is above all, and through all, and in them all.[19]

It is interesting to note, as sure as Wesley is about his doctrines and opinions, he is always open to receive a better understanding from his reading or experiences of others. We are to remain firm in our opinions until we are reasoned to a better practice or position. However, we are to respect the opinions of others who differ from us.

> Be true also to your principles touching opinions and the externals of religion. Use every ordinance which you believe is of God; but beware of narrowness of spirit towards those who use them not. Conform yourself to those modes of worship which you approve; yet love as brethren those who cannot conform. Lay so much stress on opinions, that all your own, if it be possible, may agree with truth and reason; but have a care of anger, dislike, or contempt towards those whose opinions differ from yours. You are daily accused of this; (and, indeed, what is it whereof you are not accused?) but beware of giving any ground for such an accusation. Condemn no man for not thinking as you think: Let every one enjoy the full and free liberty of thinking for himself: Let every man use his own judgment, since every man must give an account of himself to

---

[19] Wesley, *Works*, 6:396

God. Abhor every approach, in any kind or degree, to the spirit of persecution. If you cannot reason or persuade a man into the truth, never attempt to force him into it. If love will not compel him to come in, leave him to God, the Judge of all.[20]

At this early time one of the things which separated Wesley's group from the others who were also working for spiritual renewal were those who followed Wesley were Arminian. Wesley was of the theological persuasion of Arminianism, which was discussed in our chapter on prevenient grace. Another difference was they were determined to stay within the Church of England. Most of the other groups became independent from the Church of England at some point. Often, however, when they did so they were not successful in continuing as a church and gradually died out.

The next big step for Wesley was the acceptance of lay preachers who began to perform like ordained deacons within the Church of England. As time went on their duties expanded as Wesley trusted and allowed them to take on greater responsibilities.

Because of their emphasis on the sacraments or more particularly the Lord's Supper it became a problem for the Wesley's and their followers. Several different solutions were found such as using the Church of England, John and/or Charles with pastors who had regular churches, and giving communion in a building they had gotten from the Huguenots which therefore had been episcopally consecrated.

The Methodist conferences provided an opportunity for regular and lay preachers to gather and discuss problems, theology, and whatever concerns they had at the time. The conferences were started by John who saw the need to discuss theology, preaching, and the practices of these leaders. Wesley wanted the lay leaders to agree to and follow his theology and practices. If they could not agree with them they were eventually separated from the society. As their spiritual leader Wesley thought he had to maintain these things in order to fulfill his responsibilities before God to the people in his care.

It is fitting to conclude this section with a long hymn which well describes how the unity of the Church under Christ should be.

---

[20]   Wesley, *Works*, 8:357

Christ from whom all blessings flow,
Perfecting the saints below,
Hear us, who thy nature share,
Who thy mystic body are.

Join us, in one spirit join,
Let us still receive of thine'
Still for more on thee we call,
Thou, who fillest all in all.

Closer knit to thee, our Head:
Nourish us, O Christ, and feed'
Let us daily growth receive.
More and more in Jesus live.

Jesus, we thy members are:
Cherish us with kindest care:
Of thy flesh, and of thy bone,
Love, for ever love thine own!

Sweetly may we all agree,
Touch'd with softest sympathy;
Kindly for each other care:
Every member feel its share.

Wounded by the grief of one,
Now let all the members groan:
Honour'd if one member is,
All partake the common bliss.

Many are we now and one,
We who Jesus have put on:
There is neither bond nor free,
Male nor female, Lord, in thee!

Love, like death, hath all destroy'd,
Render'd all distinctions void;
Names, and sects, and parties fall"
Thou, O Christ, art all in all![21]

---

[21] Wesley, *Wesley's Hymns*, #518, vs. 1-4, 7-10

5

CHRISTIAN PERFECTION

I'm sure at times it seemed to Wesley the only ones who agreed with him on the doctrine of Christian perfection were his brother and even they disagreed on some points, and the ministers (Lay Preachers) who were in connection with him.

Because of the large body of work Wesley wrote about Christian perfection we can assume there was a need for the continual printing of his documents and providing the information required to put the doctrine in the proper perspective. Also his comments about the doctrine of Christian perfection within these writings themselves bear witness to the same story. Over the years first one group and then another seemed to take him to task over the doctrine. This was a continuing war for Wesley.

Then there were those who went to extremes such as George Bell. Wesley had to present his doctrine and guard against those who said no Christian can be perfect, we all sin, and we sin until we die as well as those who thought justification and sanctification were really the same thing and if you were justified you were obviously sanctified.

Wesley uses terms like sanctification, entire sanctification and Christian perfection somewhat alike though drawing a distinction between sanctification and complete sanctification. I will normally use the term Christian perfection to cover the final steps of sanctification which is completed or full sanctification. In this case it refers to the complete image of God being restored, or the person's life being full of the love of God and love of man, or having the mind which was in Christ.

However, Wesley's doctrine of Christian perfection is not simple even though Wesley says it is. Though some parts may be simple when the whole is put together it is complex and involves many parts and relationships to other doctrines.

We now enter the discussion of an extremely important doctrine because Wesley says that this doctrine describes a real Christian.

> Let us labour to convince all mankind, that to be a real Christian, is, to love the Lord our God with all our heart, and to serve him with all our strength; to love our neighbor as ourselves; and therefore do unto every man as we would he should do unto us.[1]

Religion itself he defines as

> Religion we conceive to be no other than love; the love of God and of all mankind; the loving God 'with all our heart, and soul, and strength,' as having 'first loved us,' as the fountain of all the good we have received, and of all we ever hope to enjoy; and the loving every soul which God hath made, every man on earth, as our own soul.[2]

Notice Wesley uses the terms religion itself and holiness as the same concept. This underscores his emphasis upon works or holiness as Christian perfection.

Wesley's doctrine of Christian perfection can be found in several places such as his sermon "On Perfection," (Works 6), "Character of a Methodist" (Works 8), "Minutes of Some Late Conversations between the Rev. Mr. Wesleys and Others" (Works 8), "The Principles of a Methodist Farther Explained" (Works 8), and naturally "A Plain Account of Christian perfection" (Works 11), followed by "Brief Thoughts on Christian perfection" (Works 11).

We will begin our discussion of this war of Wesley's by going to the tract he wrote about Christian perfection. In this tract he has gathered his completed and organized thoughts about Christian perfection and shows how his thinking has remained constant throughout the years. His thinking may have remained pretty constant but his way of presenting it

---

[1]   Wesley, *Works*, 8:472
[2]   Wesley, *Works*, 8:474

certainly matured. By looking at his long tract on Christian perfection we will be able to see how the various pieces of it fit together to form the entire doctrine. This method will also show us how this doctrine fits into his thinking about the order of salvation. Wesley's thinking about Christian perfection and his full thoughts about it begin very early in his career and continue throughout it as a very important element of his work. He wanted his doctrine to be understood because of its importance for the full Christian life. Others had forgotten, dismissed or entirely downplayed the significance of this doctrine, but to Wesley it was vital.

Wesley says reading three books influenced his thinking on Christian perfection. In 1725 he read Bishop Taylor's book "Rule and Exercises of Holy Living and Dying." In 1726 he read Thomas A Kempis' "Christian Pattern." Then a year or two later he read Law's "Christian Perfection." Finally in 1729 he began a most serious study of the Bible. This reading led him to dedicate all of his life and actions to God. He found inner religion or religion of the heart and for him from then on there is no such thing as a half Christian. You either are devoted to God or you aren't.

This study led to his sermon at St. Mary's in 1733 on "The Circumcision of the Heart," about which he wrote:

> . . . It is that habitual disposition of soul which, in the sacred writings, is termed holiness; and which directly implies, the being cleansed from sin, 'from all filthiness both of flesh and spirit;' and, by consequence, the being endued with those virtues which were in Christ Jesus; the being so 'renewed in the image of our mind,' as to be 'perfect as our Father in heaven is perfect'" . . . 'Love is the fulfilling of the law, the end of the commandment.' It is not only 'the first and great' command, but all the commandments in one. 'Whatsoever things are just, whatsoever things are pure, if there be any virtue, if there be any praise,' they are all comprised in this one word, love. In this is perfection, and glory, and happiness: The royal law of heaven and earth is this, "Thou shalt love the lord thy God with all thy heart, and with all thy soul, and with all thy mind, and with all thy strength.'[3]

---

[3]   Wesley, *Works*, 11:367-8

The conclusion of the sermon is the sum of the perfect law which is the circumcision of the heart. Though Wesley says his thought since then has not changed or wavered at the very least we will see it did at least grow in his understanding and ability to express his thoughts about it. This is another doctrine that he had to defend consistently.

When he wrote "The Character of a Methodist"[4] he is really presenting his idea of Christian Perfection as he sees it at this time. He receives very little criticism for awhile but then he is surprised to receive criticism first from Christians who say there is no such thing as Christian perfection.

About this time he is called to a meeting with the Bishop of London, Dr. Gibson, for a discussion of his doctrine of Christian perfection. Dr. Gibson approves what Wesley says about Christian perfection, and Wesley then writes and preaches his sermon on "Christian Perfection."[5]

In defining Christian perfection, Wesley says a Christian who has attained this level of the Christian life is not perfect in everything. For instance, such a person is not free from making errors of knowledge. These people do not know everything; the perfection of which Wesley speaks is not a perfection of knowledge.

> We Secondly believe, that there is no such perfection in this life, as implies an entire deliverance, either from ignorance, or mistake, in things not essential to salvation, or from manifold temptations, or from numberless infirmities, wherewith the corruptible body more or less presses down the soul.[6]

These folks can also make mistakes. Since the perfect Christians do not possess all knowledge they are open to make mistakes due to this lack. Neither does Christian perfection mean such a person is free from all infirmities. Such people may be slow thinkers, have very little imagination, and may not know all languages or even their own very well. They also may mispronounce words and may have many defects in conversation or behavior. In all these ways these who may be Perfect Christians are

---

[4]   Wesley, *Works*, 8:339-47

[5]   Wesley, *Standard Sermons*, 2:147-77

[6]   Wesley, *Works*, 11:383

not perfect and it does not matter—it has nothing to do with Christian perfection, anyway.

Then Wesley turns to an exposition of what Christian perfection does mean and in what sense we can say such Christians are perfect. After a discussion of the scriptures on this point Wesley declares Christian perfection means such a person will not commit a sin. A perfected Christian is delivered from inner as well as outer sin. This deliverance or purification is a result of their faith by accepting the gift of God's grace.

Sugden, in commenting on sermon XXXV "Christian Perfection," says Wesley's thought can be summarized from three points of view.

> He sums it up from three points of view as (1) Purity of intention, dedicating all the life to God; (2) All the mind which was in Christ, enabling us to walk as Christ walked; the renewal of the heart in the whole image of God; (3) Loving God with all our heart, and our neighbor as ourselves; in other words, Full Consecration, Entire Sanctification, Perfect Love.[7]

This must be the simple part of Wesley's doctrine of Christian perfection. We will find that he will follow one or more of these descriptions of Christian perfection in all his work. These Christians are no longer apart from Christ because they have within them the mind which was in Christ. God has acted and saved them from all idols and cleaned them. They are able to walk in the light as Christ walked in the light. Wesley says such a person can now say Christ lives within him.

> We mean one in whom is 'the mind which was in Christ,' and who so 'walketh as Christ also walked;' a man 'that, hath clean hands and a pure heart,' or that is 'cleansed from all filthiness of flesh and spirit;' one in whom is 'no occasion of stumbling,' and who, accordingly, 'does not commit sin.' To declare this a little more particularly: We understand by that scriptural expression, 'a perfect man,' one in whom God hath fulfilled his faithful word, 'From all your filthiness and from all your idols I will cleanse you: I will also save you from all your uncleannesses.' We understand hereby, one whom God hath 'sanctified throughout

---

[7] Wesley, *Standard Sermons*, 2:148, also Works, 11:444

> in body, soul, and spirit;' one who 'walketh in the light as He
> is in the light, in whom is no darkness at all; the blood of Jesus
> Christ his Son having cleansed him from all sin.'[8]

The love of God infuses their life which has now become a life totally dedicated to God. The Christian begins as a new born or a babe in Christ. Others are more mature Christians. Some Christians are babes in Christ and as such may be perfect in some sense. They are perfect in the sense they do not commit sin. This babe in Christ is justified, he may feel the desire to sin, i.e., pride, lust, or anger but he does not give in to that sin. The Christian who is perfected or sanctified does not even feel the desire to sin.

Now this is a difficult proposition for humans to consider. How indeed does a man, or even a Christian, not feel the desire to sin? Something more powerful than the sinful desire must be within us which takes its place, shoves it out of our awareness, and whatever does this must be extremely powerful. Only the love of God is strong enough to achieve this remarkable transformation in man.

We will now relate Christian perfection to nine other doctrines or concepts. In order to do so we will often use the comparison between justification and sanctification to more clearly describe what Christian perfection entails which is different or unique or sometimes similar but not the same.

A. CHRISTIAN PERFECTION AND JUSTIFICATION BY FAITH

Wesley answers the perplexing question of where to place Christian perfection or sanctification in the order of salvation by saying Christian perfection or entire sanctification begins when a person is justified. It cannot start before justification because it is a deeper and richer step in the Christian life.

> Justification is another word for pardon. It is the forgiveness of all
> our sins; and what is necessarily implied therein, our acceptance

---

8   Wesley, *Works*, 11:384

with God. The price whereby this hath been procured for us (commonly termed 'the meritorious cause of our justification'), is the blood and righteousness of Christ; or, to express it a little more clearly, all that Christ hath done and suffered for us, til He 'poured out His soul for the transgressors.' The immediate effects of justification are, the peace of God, a 'peace that passeth all understanding' and a 'rejoicing in hope of the glory of God' 'with joy unspeakable and full of glory.'[9]

Normally sanctification or the growth toward Christian perfection begins at justification but is not completed at that time because the love of God and man has not yet taken full possession of the Christian. This is usually a process, a process of gradually dying to sin and growing in the acceptance of God's grace.

Justification is an acceptance of God's grace that your sins are forgiven. This is preceded by the prevenient grace of God which leads one to repentance and then acceptance of God's gift in Christ for our forgiveness. Logically the full opening of the life to the love of God and having the mind in you which was in Christ must follow justification. Christian perfection (entire sanctification) is a result of growth which starts at justification and hopefully continues. They are not the same and they cannot be reversed; Christian perfection does not come before justification.

Since Wesley believed man must be made perfect before he can see God, and since man even most of the Christians we know are not perfect in love, there must be a time at which the normal Christian is made perfect. Wesley says this usually is a gift of God's grace that is received by the Christian at the point of death.

> We grant, (1.) That many of those who have died in the faith, yea, the greater part of those we have known, were not perfected in love till a little before their death. (2.) That the term *sanctified* is continually applied by St. Paul to all that were justified. (3.) That by this term alone he rarely, if ever, means 'saved from all sin.' (4.) That consequently, it is not proper to use it in that sense, without adding the word *wholly, entirely,* or the like. (5.) That the inspired writers almost continually speak of or

---

[9] Wesley, *Standard Sermons,* 2:445-6

to those who were justified, but very rarely of or to those who were wholly sanctified. (6.) That, consequently, it behoves us to speak almost continually of the state of justification; but more rarely, at least in full and explicit terms, concerning entire sanctification.'[10]

Some say it is impossible for man to receive Christian perfection before the point of death. They say man is a sinner and therefore cannot be made perfect before then. Wesley denies this perception of Christianity and Christian perfection.

He believes God has given us the command to be holy. Christian perfection is a gift of God but it is received by faith. One reason we hear so little about this is because we have forgotten that the Christian faith is a process of growth in our relationship with God. This growth is not just pointed in any direction as if we could grow with God in many ways, their being multiple ends towards which God is pulling us. This growth is to lead us to Christian perfection, and achieving that perfection while we are yet alive.

Justification and sanctification are the two parts or major doctrines of salvation. The Christian first comes to justification and normally much later, through a process of Christian growth, the Christian may come to complete or full sanctification or Christian perfection. Most, unfortunately, do not make it this far until near death. More unfortunately still, many are not even aware they can or should seek after it during this life.

Sanctification begins at the very moment of justification and though both of them (justification and Christian perfection) could be given at the same time by God's grace, they usually aren't.

B. Christian Perfection and Repentance

It is interesting though not surprising to find repentance remains a part of the Christians life, even in the perfected Christians life. Even though the Christian has been justified by faith and has now reached Christian perfection, there is still a place for repentance.

---

10   Wesley, *Works*, 11:388

In Wesley we find two types of repentance. The first is what is often called legal repentance. This is the type of repentance which is found at the start of the Christian life. The acceptance of God's prevenient grace leads to this initial repentance.

> To be deeply sensible of this, (our sins and thus our condition before God) how helpless thou art, as well as how guilty and how sinful,—this is that 'repentance not to be repented of,' which is the forerunner of the kingdom of God. [Parenthesis mine]
>
> 7. If to this lively conviction of thy inward and outward sins, of thy utter guiltiness and helplessness, there be added suitable affections,—sorrow of heart, for having despised thy own mercies; remorse, and self-condemnation, having thy mouth stopped; shame to lift up thine eyes to heaven; fear of the wrath of God abiding on thee, of His curse hanging over thy head, and of the fiery indignation ready to devour those who forget God, and obey not our Lord Jesus Christ; earnest desire to escape from that indignation, to cease from evil, and learn to do well,—then I say unto thee, in the name of the Lord, 'Thou art not far from the kingdom of God.' One step more, and thou shalt enter in. Thou dost 'repent.' Now, 'believe the gospel.'[11]

This repentance is at the gate of religion and is a conviction we have that we are sinful, helpless, and full of guilt. This repentance goes before we receive the Kingdom of God which is really within us.

This particular repentance is a type of self-knowledge in which we now know ourselves as sinners, guilty, and helpless before God even though we have become children of God. This repentance comes before faith and convicts us as a sinner and what type of sinner. The sinner knows he is far from original righteousness and the image of God. The sinner becomes aware he is corrupted and corrupted in his relationship with God. The sinner's will is not God's will—it is instead perverse. The love of this sinner is found to be directed away from God towards idols or anything except God. There is then no soundness in the spiritual side of this sinner.

---

[11]   Wesley, *Standard Sermons*, 1:158-9

Wesley also finds repentance as a part of the Christian life after justification or as one strives for Christian perfection. In fact there is no time in the Christian experience one can leave repentance behind to just grow in the Christian life without it.

Even after accepting God's grace and becoming a child of God, after being justified by faith and being aware of the witness of God with our spirits that we are his children, we still feel sin within us.

We feel pride stirring and we begin to think more highly of ourselves than we should. We feel self-will and this will is often contrary to God's will for our lives. This self-will is a part of man, says Wesley, and we cannot get rid of it. We do not always, like Jesus, submit our wills to God.

Wesley says this self-will and pride are no more or no less than idolatry because we have placed something where God should be in our lives. This is contrary to our loving God and man as we ought.

We begin to feel all the things we used to feel when we were not children of God. We may begin to feel the desire to love the creature more than the creator, we may feel the pull of the desire of the eye which is the great or beautiful, we may begin to feel the pride of life, or fear of the distaste of others. Then jealousies may arise and we may begin to covet what others have. We may begin backsliding, which is Wesley's term for our readiness to depart from our relationship with God. We may also engage in uncharitable conversation which does not proceed from our love of man. Again our actions: though the world may applaud some or many of them we are not unaware of the sin which cleaves to these actions. We and only we may know and be aware of those mixed reasons for action—but we do know. Then again, what of the sins of omission? How many times are we not truly following God's will and decide not to act when we should? Instead of the mixed actions (good, sinful) we have the mixed reasons for our inaction.

With Wesley there is a second repentance and this repentance comes after the repentance which comes before justification. This repentance and indeed faith, comes after justification which allows the Christian to grow in faith and to continue in the faith.

> But, notwithstanding this, there is also a repentance and a faith (taking the words in another sense, a sense not quite the same, nor yet entirely different) which are requisite after we

have 'believed the gospel'; yea, and in every subsequent stage of the Christian course, or we cannot 'run the race which is set before us.' And this repentance and faith are full as necessary, in order to our *continuance* and *growth* in grace, as the former faith and repentance were, in order to our *entering* into the kingdom of God.[12]

This repentance has to do with growing beyond justification because one cannot go further in the Christian life until one does. We are aware that sin still is within us; the root has not been destroyed. This requires a second or further grace which removes even the root of sin from us. The Christian believes in the promises which God has made. Not only do we believe in the promises of God but we also believe God will perform in us the promises which He has made.

Know this. We are all guilty of these sins and cannot escape from them.

Thus it is, that in the children of God, repentance and faith exactly answer each other. By repentance we feel the sin remaining in our hearts, and cleaving to our words and actions: by faith, we receive the power of God in Christ, purifying our hearts, and cleansing our hands. By repentance, we are still sensible that we deserve punishment for all our tempers and words, and actions; by faith, we are conscious that our Advocate with the Father is continually pleading for us, and thereby continually turning aside all condemnation and punishment from us. By repentance we have an abiding conviction that there is not help in us: by faith we receive not only mercy, 'but grace to help in' *every* 'time of need.' Repentance disclaims the very possibility of any other help: faith accepts all the help we stand in need of, from Him that hath all power in heaven and earth. Repentance says, 'Without Him I can do nothing': faith says, 'I can do all things through Christ strengthening me.' Through Him I can not only overcome, but expel, all the enemies of my soul. Through Him I can 'love the Lord my God with all my heart, mind, souls, and strength'; yea, and

---

[12]   Wesley, *Standard Sermons*, 2:380

'walk in holiness and righteousness before Him all the days of my life.'[13]

This repentance comes in the process of sanctification or Christian perfection. Since, as we will find out, Wesley believes most of us are perfected at the moment of our deaths, this repentance likewise may come then. However, there is no need to wait until then for us to seek Christian perfection. One of the first steps is by God's grace, to become aware of our continued sinfulness and to respond with our repentance for this sinfulness. This repentance is called by some "evangelical" to distinguish and separate it from the original repentance, called legal repentance which we discussed earlier and which we felt when we first began our walk with God.

C. Christian Perfection and the New Birth

John Wesley believed justification by faith and the New Birth were the foundation for Christianity. Justification is the great work God does for us by forgiving us our sins and the new birth is the great work God does in us by reversing our fallen nature. As far as when they happen in the Christian life, they come at the same time but if we were to logically think about them we would think of justification first and then the new birth.

Wesley relates the new birth to the doctrine of original sin. Man was originally created in the image of God but since the fall we no longer have the full image of God within us. Therefore, in order for the image of God to be restored in us we must be born again, born in the spirit of God. Because Adam fell and we are his children born after the fall, we reap the results of the fall.

> And in Adam all died, all human kind, all the children of men who were then in Adam's loins. The natural consequence of this is, that every one descended from him comes into the world spiritually dead, dead to God, wholly dead in sin; entirely void of the life of God; void of the image of God, of all that

---

13   Wesley, *Standard Sermons*, 2:394

righteousness and holiness wherein Adam was created. Instead of this, every man born into the world now bears the image of the devil, in pride and self-will; the image of the beast, in sensual appetites and desires. This, then, is the foundation of the new birth,—the entire corruption of our nature. Hence it is, that being born in sin, we must be 'born again.' Hence every one that is born of a woman must be born in the Spirit of God.[14]

In other words, when we are born in this life we are born apart from God with his image gone or distorted. Just as a child in the womb has eyes but cannot see the outside world, so we are blind to the things of God and cannot hear his Word. Such a person has no knowledge of God either spiritual or eternal because he has no spiritual senses with which to receive such knowledge. As Wesley says "though he is a living man he is a dead Christian."[15] When we are awakened to the things of God our spiritual eyes are opened and the light and love of God can shine through.

This then, is the new birth:

It is that great change which God works in the soul when He brings it into life; when He raises it from the death of sin to the life of righteousness. It is the change wrought in the whole soul by the almighty Spirit of God when it is 'created anew in Christ Jesus'; when it is 'renewed after the image of God in righteousness and true holiness'; when the love of the world is changed into the love of God; pride into humility; passion into meekness; hatred, envy, malice, into a sincere, tender, disinterested love for all mankind. In a word, it is that change whereby the earthly sensual devilish mind is turned into the 'mind which was in Christ Jesus.' This is the nature of the new birth: 'so is every one that is born of the Spirit.'[16]

This new birth comes at the same moment as justification and begins the process of Christian living.

---

[14] Wesley, *Standard Sermons* 2:230-1
[15] Wesley, *Standard Sermons*, 2:233
[16] Wesley, *Standard Sermons*, 2:234

There is also another sense or use of the new birth which is a regeneration, or change in our lives which accompanies Christian perfection. The new birth is necessary for us to receive holiness which is having the image of God stamped on our hearts or the whole mind of Christ in us. The holiness is given to us by God's grace. Holiness cannot begin to be within us until God's grace gives it to us.

The one (first) accompanies our change from natural man or sinner to accepting God's grace, repenting, and becoming justified by faith. At this very moment our lives are changed or reordered.

The other (second) accompanies our moving into the process of sanctification or Christian perfection towards one of the last steps, in fact next to last step if we consider death and glorification to be the final step. It is not the same as Christian perfection though some would confuse the two and think they are the same. This new birth is not to be confused with the whole of Christian perfection; it is only the gate or door to it.

God's grace and love are pulling us, cajoling us towards this Christian perfection and just like the new birth which accompanies justification; there is one which accompanies Christian perfection.

> Q. When may a person judge himself to have attained this? (Christian Perfection)[Parenthesis mine.]
> A. When, after having been fully convinced of inbred sin, by a far deeper and clearer conviction than that he experienced before justification, and after having experienced a gradual mortification of it, he experiences a total death to sin, and an entire renewal in the love and image of God, so as to rejoice evermore, to pray without ceasing, and in everything to give thanks. Not that 'to feel all love and no sin' is a sufficient proof. Several have experienced this for a time, before their souls were fully renewed. None therefore ought to believe that the work is done, till there is added the testimony of the Spirit, witnessing his entire sanctification, as clearly as his justification.[17]

This process is a renewal of the image of God within us and is a change which is even greater than the original new birth because now not just the sins are gone as in justification, now the root of sin out of which all

---

[17]   Wesley, *Works*, 11:401-2

sins come has been removed and the love of God and man reigns in the person.

This dual concept of new birth is as necessary as it is strange to many of us. It is necessary because if one is changed or renewed from a justified life, wherein we still struggle with sin and find it working its way through our actions and in our actions, to a sanctified life in which these things are gone because the root of pride and self-will are now gone, this change is a great one and needs to be understood by the average Christian as something to be prayed and worked for.

This regeneration or "new birth" may well come to us at the point of death but Wesley asks us, why not now? Indeed, why not?

D. CHRISTIAN PERFECTION AND ASSURANCE

If repentance is of two kinds, we find in Wesley two kinds of assurance as well. The first assurance is the assurance which we may receive when we begin the Christian life. This assurance contains not only the awareness of forgiveness for our sins but also awareness we are children of God. Not only is this true but there is also a dual witness: the witness of our spirits and the witness of the Spirit of God.

Wesley points to the witness of our spirit as our seeing the fruits in our life of faith, hope, and love and our following the commandments of God. Also, since our conscience, though natural in one respect, is a gift of God on the other, and if our conscience follows the commandments of God, we know we have the testimony of our spirit.

The Spirit of God testifies to us we are children of God and the fruit of this Spirit is love, joy, peace, longsuffering, gentleness, and goodness. The witness of the Spirit comes before the witness of our spirit because there can be no fruits of the spirit before the Spirit gives them. It is only after the witness of the Spirit we can have the witness in our spirits; because we can see the fruits of the Spirit within our lives.

Now let's look at the assurance in sanctification or Christian perfection. We know we are sanctified or made perfect as a Christian by the witness of the Spirit and by the fruits of the Spirit. In other words, we know it in the same way we know we are justified.

When we were justified the Spirit bore witness to us our sins were forgiven; now in sanctification or Christian perfection the Spirit bears witness to us our sins are taken away. This witness is not always clear and sometimes it is stronger than at other times. Indeed, it may even be withdrawn from us at times.

> Q. 16. But how do you know that you are sanctified, saved from your inbred corruption?
> A. I can know it no otherwise than I know that I am justified. 'Hereby know we that we are of God,' in either sense, 'by the Spirit that he hath given us.'

> "We know it by the witness and by the fruit of the Spirit. And, First, by the witness. As, when we were justified, the Spirit bore witness with our spirit, that our sins were forgiven; so, when we were sanctified, he bore witness, that they were taken away. Indeed, the witness of sanctification is not always clear at first; (as neither is that of justification;) neither is it afterward always the same, but, like that of justification, sometimes stronger and sometimes fainter. Yea, and sometimes it is withdrawn. Yet, in general, the latter testimony of the Spirit is both as clear and as steady as the former.[18]

Wesley draws a distinction between the witness of the fruit of the Spirit in justification and sanctification by the constancy of our resigning our wills to God's will. In sanctification there is the constancy which is missing in justification. The fruits of the Spirit in Christian perfection are many: love, joy, peace, always with us—longsuffering, patience, and resignation—gentleness rising over all provocation—goodness, and mildness—fidelity, simplicity—meekness, calmness—temperance in all things.

One may say the same thing is true of justification, but it really is not true. We may see some of these witnesses but in justification we still have the root of sin, which are pride, and self-will, still evident and we know they are still there. In sanctification or Christian perfection they are gone.

---

18 Wesley, *Works*, 11:420

Q. 23. But what great matter is there in this? Have we not all this when we are justified?

A. What, total resignation to the will of God, without any mixture of self-will? gentleness, without any touch of anger, even the moment we are provoked? love to God, without the least love to the creature, but in and for God, excluding all pride? Love to man, excluding all envy, all jealousy, and rash judging? meekness, keeping the whole soul inviolably calm? and temperance in all things? Deny that any ever came up to this, if you please; but do not say, all who are justified do.[19]

So we have a dual witness of the Spirit and this witness is of two kinds. In both we can see the fruits of the Spirit in our lives. In the witness of the Spirit the witness is of two different things. In justification it is a witness that we are saved from sins and therefore are justified and in sanctification or Christian perfection we have the witness that the root of sin has been pulled and by the grace of God it is gone.

One of the Wesley's hymns says it so well:

> How can a sinner know
> His sins on earth forgiven?
> How can my gracious Saviour show
> My name transcribed in heaven?
> What we have felt and seen,
> With confidence we tell;
> And publish to the sons of men
> The signs infallible.
>
> We who in Christ believe
> That be for us he hath died.
> We all his unknown peace receive,
> And feel his blood applied;
> Exults our rising soul,
> Disburden'd of her load,
> And swells unutterably full
> Of glory and of God.

---

19   Wesley, *Works*, 11:422-3

We by his Spirit prove
And know the things of God,
The things which freely of his love
He hath on us bestow'd:
His Spirit to us he gave,
And dwells in us, we know:
The witness in ourselves we have,
And all its fruits we show.

The meek and lowly heart
That in our Saviour was,
To us his Spirit doth impart,
And signs us with his cross:
Our nature's turn'd, our mind
Transform'd in all its powers;
And both the Witnesses are join'd,
The Spirit of God with ours.[20]

E. Christian Perfection and Faith

As we have earlier pointed out Wesley believed we are justified by faith by the grace of God. We also remember sanctification begins at the same time. Wesley says faith is the only condition for man to be justified.

> And, first, how are we justified by faith? In what sense is this to be understood? I answer, Faith is the condition, and the only condition of justification. It is the *condition*: none is justified but he that believes: without faith no man is justified. And it is the *only condition*: this alone is sufficient for justification. Every one that believes is justified, whatever else he has or has not. In other words: no man is justified till he believes: every man when he believes is justified.[21]

But what then does he have to say about sanctification? What about faith there? Or, does one just automatically grow into sanctification? As

---

[20]   Wesley, *Wesley's Hymns*, #96, vs. 1,2,4,5

[21]   Wesley, *Standard Sermons*, 2:451

justification has faith as its single condition so also Christian perfection has faith as its single condition.

Some in Wesley's day said he promoted works as a necessary work of man in order for him to be justified but he does not agree with their interpretation. Just as faith alone is the condition for justification so it is the single condition for sanctification.

> Exactly as we are justified by faith, so are we sanctified by faith. Faith is the condition, and the only condition, of sanctification, exactly as it is of justification. It is the *condition*: none is sanctified but he that believes: without faith no man is sanctified. And it is the *only condition*: this alone is sufficient for sanctification. Every one that believes is sanctified, whatever else he has or has not. In other words, no man is sanctified till he believes: every man when he believes is sanctified. [22]

The faith Wesley talks about is not an intellectual agreement with a proposition because even the devils or the devil knows about God. More is required than mere intellectual acceptance of the proposition God is and God does. Religion is a matter of the heart and as such is a full, complete, and total reliance upon Christ that the Father's work through the Son has indeed performed the saving work for me, even me, which the scripture describes.

This faith is an ability, God given, to have our eyes opened to things spiritual and we can begin to see those things which before we and the world thought were strange and foolish for one to believe and not only now believe, but also to trust our lives to its truth. We can now see the truth of religion and what the world sees as folly and a broken reed.

The content of this faith is defined by Wesley in his Standard Sermon "Salvation by Faith."

> . . . It acknowledges His death as the only sufficient means of redeeming man from death eternal, and His resurrection as the restoration of us all to life and immortality; inasmuch as He 'was delivered for our sins, and rose again for our justification.' Christian faith is, then, not only an assent to the whole gospel

---

[22] Wesley, *Standard Sermons*, 2:453

of Christ, but also a full reliance on the blood of Christ; a trust in the merits of His life, death, and resurrection: a recumbency upon Him as our atonement and our life, *as given for us*, and *living in us*. [It is a sure confidence which a man hath in God, that through the merits of Christ, *his* sins are forgiven, and *he* reconciled to the favour of God:] and, in consequence hereof, a closing with Him, and cleaving to Him as our 'wisdom, righteousness, sanctification, and redemption,' or, in one word, our salvation.[23]

So faith is really the act of the whole person in response to the act of God in Christ and what God therefore has done for us which we could not do for ourselves.

> Into thy gracious hands I fall,
> And with the arms of faith embrace;
> O King of Glory, hear my call;
> O raise me, heal me, by thy grace!
> Now righteousness through thy wounds I am;
> No condemnation now I dread;
> I taste salvation in thy name,
> Alive in thee, my living Head.
>
> Still let thy wisdom be my guide,
> Nor take thy light from me away:
> Still with me let thy grace abide,
> That I from thee may never stray:
> Let thy word richly in me dwell;
> Thy peace and love my portion be;
> My joy to' endure and do thy will,
> Till perfect I am found in thee.
>
> Arm me with thy whole armour, Lord!
> Support my weakness with thy might;
> Gird on my thigh thy conquering sword,
> And shield me in the threatening fight:
> From faith to faith, from grace to grace,
> So in thy strength shall I go on;

---

[23] Wesley, *Standard Sermons*, 1:40-41

Till heaven and earth flee from thy face,
And glory end what grace begun.[24]

F. CHRISTIAN PERFECTION AND THE MORAL LAW

Like the other terms which relate to Christian perfection, the Law comes before Christian perfection but it also has a role in Christian perfection.

The first time we run into the Law is when it is used to convince us of our sin and therefore of the distance we are from the holy and righteous God. Though we have been able to relate to others, often in an effectual way, we have no way of cajoling, pleading or somehow making God be attentive to us and force him to have a relationship with us. We have nothing to give, no way to force him, no way to bring us together because the Law shows us how far we are apart from him.

As Wesley puts it:

> . . . the uses of the law. And the first use of it, without question, is, to convince the world of sin. This is, indeed, the peculiar work of the Holy Ghost: who can work it without any means at all, or by whatever means it pleaseth Him, however insufficient in themselves, or even improper, to produce such an effect. And, accordingly, some there are whose hearts have been broken in pieces in a moment, either in sickness or in health, without any visible cause, or any outward means whatever; and others (one in an age) have been awakened to a sense of the 'wrath of God abiding on them,' by hearing that 'God was in Christ, reconciling the world unto Himself.' But it is the ordinary method of the Spirit of God to convict sinners by the law. It is this which, being set home on the conscience, generally breaketh the rocks in pieces . . . . By this is the sinner discovered to himself. All his fig-leaves are torn away, and he sees that he is 'wretched, and poor, and miserable, and blind, and naked.' The law flashes conviction on every side. He feels

---

24 Wesley, *Wesley's Hymns*, #196

himself a mere sinner. He has nothing to pay. His 'mouth is stopped,' and he stands 'guilty before God.'[25]

This is the first use of the law, but we now speak of those who are much farther along in the Christian life. Since we are justified by faith is there really any further use of the law? Can't we now say because of God's love and the sacrifice of Christ we are brought into a love relationship and since we are not trying to be accepted by God because of our good works of the law but by our faith we no longer need the law—we have outgrown the law? 'Thank goodness, we think, we didn't want to worry any more about the law, its meanings, and consequences.

However, if this is what we think Wesley says we are very much mistaken. He has a very positive use of the law for us as mature and maturing Christians.

Wesley's concept is that the first use of the law is to get us to justification. This use of the law convinces us of our sin, and as such we are dead to God. We are physically alive but have no spiritual life because we are dead in our trespasses to sin.

The use of the law we talk about when we discuss Christian perfection is the law which keeps us alive. By this Wesley means the law prepares us for further work of God within us. This particular function of the law, Wesley believes, is not well known or understood by even the Christians of his day. Many of them think since they are justified by faith there is no longer any reason for them to think further about the law or even to follow it.

Wesley agrees in one sense we are done with the law, at least the Jewish ceremonial law, even the entire Mosaic dispensation and even further, we do not need the moral law as a means of receiving our justification, since it was by faith. The law is, however, of use to those who are on the path to Christian perfection.

The law is able to show us the sin which still remains in our lives, in receiving the strength and resources from Christ to allow us to follow his law. The law also confirms even though we are not able to attain it all,

---

[25]   Wesley, *Standard Sermons*, 2:52

we may still receive grace upon grace from Christ until we can have his promises fulfilled in us.[26]

The law we are now under is the law of faith. We are under this law to God and to Christ, our creator and redeemer. Love is the fulfilling of this law. Faith working by love is what God requires of us now. Love is the end of every commandment God has given us. The foundation may be faith, and indeed it is, but the end or goal is love.

The love we are talking about is the law of God and neighbor and the fruits of this law are as follows:

> Q. 7. What are the fruits of properties of this love?
> A. St. Paul informs us at large, love is long-suffering. It suffers all the weaknesses of the children of God, all the wickedness of the children of the world; and that not for a little time only, but as long as God pleases. In all, it sees the hand of God, and willingly submits thereto. Meantime, it is kind. In all, and after all, it suffers, it is soft, mild, tender, benign. 'Love envieth not;' it excludes every kind and degree of envy out of the heart: 'love acteth not rashly,' in a violent, headstrong manner, nor passes any rash or severe judgment: It 'doth not behave itself indecently;' is not rude, does not act out of character; 'Seeketh not her own' ease, pleasure, honour, or profit: 'Is not provoked;' expels all anger from the heart: 'Thinketh no evil;' casteth out all jealousy, suspiciousness, and readiness to believe evil: 'Rejoiceth not in iniquity;' yea, weeps at the sin or folly of its bitterest enemies: 'But rejoiceth in the truth;' in the holiness and happiness of every child of man. 'Love covereth all things,' speaks evil of no man; 'believeth all things' that tend to the advantage of another's character. It 'hopeth all things,' whatever may extenuate the faults which cannot be denied; and it 'endureth all things' which God can permit, or men and devils inflict. This is the 'law of Christ, the perfect law, the law of liberty.'[27]

Wesley draws a distinction, then, between the law of faith and the law of works. The law of faith is love and the law of works is the same law

---

[26] Wesley, *Standard Sermons*, 2:54-55

[27] Wesley, *Works*, 11:416

we cannot fulfill to be justified by God. The Wesley's and the Methodists sang about this law.

> The thing my God doth hate
> That I no more may do,
> Thy creature, Lord, again create,
> And all my soul renew:
> My soul shall then, like thine,
> Abhor the thing unclean,
> And sanctified by love divine,
> For ever cease from sin.
>
> That blessed law of thine,
> Jesus, to me impart:
> The Spirit's law of life divine,
> O write it in my heart!
> Implant it deep within,
> Whence it may ne'er remove;
> The law of liberty from sin,
> The perfect law of love.
>
> Thy nature be my law,
> Thy spotless sanctity,
> And sweetly every moment draw
> My happy soul to thee.
> Soul of my soul remain!
> Who didst for all fulfil,
> In me, O Lord, fulfil again
> Thy heavenly Father's will[28]

G. Christian Perfection and Sin

We all know there is sin in our lives before we become Christians. Or, to put it another way, there is sin in our lives before we believe or have faith in Christ and rely totally on him for our salvation. This is called justification or justification by faith by the grace of God.

---

[28] Wesley, *Wesley's Hymns*, #340

The next question is, is there sin in our lives once we have been justified? Wesley breaks sin into two parts, inward and outward sin. As far as outward sin is concerned the justified do not have it because those who perform outward sins are not children of God. In his sermon "On Sin in Believers" Wesley writes:

> By sin, I here understand inward sin; any sinful temper, passion, or affection; such as pride, self-will, love of the world in any kind or degree; such as lust, anger, peevishness; any disposition contrary to the mind which was in Christ.
>
> 3. The question is not concerning *outward sin*; whether a child of God *commit sin* or no. We all agree and earnestly maintain, 'He that committeth sin is of the devil. 'We agree, 'Whosoever is born of God does not commit sin.'[29]

The justified person is in a wonderful position because they have been born again. The Christian who has been perfected has power over inward and outward sin from the moment of justification which as we remember is also the beginning part of sanctification.

Wesley discusses the problem of sin in believers from the point of view there are two principles in man. These principles are our nature and grace or to put it another way, flesh and spirit. We are led to fight against one even as they both are warring in our lives.

> Let us, therefore, hold fast the sound doctrine 'once delivered to the saints,' and delivered down by them, with the written words, to all succeeding generations: that, although we are renewed, cleansed, purified, sanctified, the moment we truly believe in Christ, yet we are not then renewed, cleansed, purified altogether; but the flesh, the evil nature, still *remains* (though subdued), and wars against the Spirit. So much the more let us use all diligence in 'fighting the good fight of faith.' So much the more earnestly let us 'watch and pray' against the enemy within. The more carefully let us take to ourselves, and 'put on, the whole armour of God'; that, although 'we wrestle' both 'with flesh and blood, and with principalities, and powers,

---

29 Wesley, *Standard Sermons*, 2:365

and wicked spirits in high places,' we 'may be able to withstand in the evil day, and having done all, to stand.'[30]

As far as Christian perfection is concerned there is sin and sin of two kinds. At the start of Christian perfection or sanctification or the Christian life, outer sin is gone but inner sin remains. Only of the fully perfected Christian can we say they are free from evil thoughts and tempers and from evil or sinful thoughts. Only of these fully perfected Christians can we say pride has been conquered, and along with these, self-will, and anger.

Wesley does admit Christian perfection is not static. There is no level or state in which growth can stop and the Christian be satisfied with his progress. Growth occurs before Christian perfection and continues after Christian perfection.

> Yet we may, lastly, observe, that neither in this respect is there any absolute perfection on earth. There is no *perfection of degrees*, as it is termed; none which does not admit of a continual increase. So that how much soever any man has attained, or in how high a degree soever he is perfect, he hath still need to 'grow in grace,' and daily to advance in the knowledge and love of God his Saviour.[31]

Wesley is sure there is growth in Christian perfection.[32] Since sanctification or Christian perfection is to be a restoral of the image of God, the image is filled with righteousness and true holiness. And, since a perfect Christian is one who loves God with heart, soul, and mind, we can say that all inward sin is taken away. Sin remains even in the Christian who is growing in perfection until he is fully sanctified throughout. When fully sanctified, sin begins to die in this mature Christian and the Christian grows in God's grace.

There is one other source of sin in Christian perfection and one could easily miss this understanding. Even though Wesley says they are not really sins by his definition of a conscious, deliberate act, sin may still result from them.

---

[30] Wesley *Standard Sermons*, 2:378
[31] Wesley, *Standard Sermons*, 2:156
[32] Wesley, *Works*, 11:374

The argument runs this way: One who has been given Christian perfection is still liable to mistakes. These mistakes may lead one to a mistake in practice. Such a mistake may be a transgression of the law and lead such a person to be eligible for damnation. However, since the mistake is done from love, the mercies of Christ may be relied upon to remove such unknown mistakes as an obstacle to salvation.

> To explain myself a little farther on this head: (1.) Not only sin, properly so called, (that is, a voluntary transgression of a known law,) but sin, improperly so called, (that is, an involuntary transgression of a divine law, known or unknown,) needs the atoning blood. (2.) I believe there is no such perfection in this life as excludes these involuntary transgressions which I apprehend to be naturally consequent on the ignorance and mistakes inseparable from mortality. (3.) Therefore *sinless perfection* is a phrase I never use, lest I should seem to contradict myself. (4.) I believe a person filled with the love of God is still liable to these involuntary transgressions. (5.) Such transgressions you may call sins, if you please: I do not, for the reasons above-mentioned.[33]

H. CHRISTIAN PERFECTION AND WORKS (GOOD AND NOT SO GOOD)

The place or lack of place for works in the Christian life has been debated for a long time in the Christian community. Good Christians have seen it differently over all these years. Are works necessary and if so, at what stage of the Christian life and for what reason are they considered good? Or, are works wrong, evil or just plain unnecessary to the Christian life and in fact are a way of trying to save yourself in God's eyes by your attempts at good works?

In the Wesleyan scheme there is always an emphasis upon "fruits" or works. His emphasis upon Christian living and the fruits of Christian living or holiness is a great part of his understanding of what it means for one to be Christian.

---

[33] Wesley, *Works*, 11:396

Works must be understood as an element in Christian living from the start, even before one becomes a Christian, though these works have nothing to do with justification, in the sense faith alone is necessary for justification.

Wesley was much misunderstood in his day as well as ours in his emphasis upon works. When he speaks about works prior to justification, but which are brought about due to repentance he calls them both good and bad. Is anybody surprised at this twist in Wesley's theology? They were bad in the sense they were not strictly good works because they did not come from justification or from salvation. On the other hand, these works were in a sense necessary for salvation because they were a result of the repentance which precedes justification.

Though these works are before justification they are a response to the convincing grace of God and therefore are not to be confused in any sense with a human merit which makes man acceptable in the sight of God. Man is justified by faith alone through God's grace alone.

As man becomes convinced and becomes repentant, he responds to the convincing grace of God, pulling and urging him to keep growing.

> God does undoubtedly command us both to repent, and to bring forth fruits meet for repentance: which if we willingly neglect, we cannot reasonably expect to be justified at all: therefore both repentance, and fruits meet for repentance, are, in some sense, necessary to justification. But they are not necessary in the *same sense* with faith, nor in the *same degree*. Not in the *same degree*; for those fruits are only necessary *conditionally*; if there be time and opportunity for them. Otherwise a man may be justified without them . . . [34]

Now however, we speak of works for repentance prior to entire Christian perfection or entire sanctification. These works are good works since they do not arise from prevenient grace but the sanctifying grace of God. If there is time for the Christian between being given Christian perfection and their death, good works must be present in their life or they will not reach full sanctification or Christian perfection. These works arise in the Christian's life but they do not take the place of faith in Christian

---

[34] Wesley, *Standard Sermons*, 2:451-452

perfection. In other words, we are not justified by faith through grace and then sanctified by works. We are sanctified by faith through God's grace as well.

These works are divided into two types. The first concerns our relationship with God and our response to his grace. They are called works of piety and include prayers, reading the Scripture, partaking of communion, and fasting or abstaining as our bodies are able.

The second type of works concerns our relationship with our fellow man, who we are to love, and includes loving our neighbors in a way which nurtures both their bodies and their souls. These works include such things as feeding the hungry, clothing the naked, entertaining the stranger, visiting those who are ill or in prison, instructing the ignorant, awakening the sinner, helping rekindle the fires of those who are lukewarm, and contributes in many ways to help souls from spiritual death.

For full salvation, Christian perfection, Wesley says fruits (works) are necessary yet they are not necessary in the same sense as faith. The fruits are remotely necessary in the sense they help us to continue to grow in our Christian life. The fruits may not come because our life may end before there is time of opportunity for them. They are important, but faith is necessary.

> Though it be allowed, that both this repentance and its fruits are necessary to full salvation; yet they are not necessary either in the same sense with faith, or in the same degree,—Not in the *same degree*; for these fruits are only necessary *conditionally*, if there be time and opportunity for them; otherwise a man may be sanctified without them. But he cannot be sanctified without faith. Likewise, lest a man have ever so much of this repentance, or ever so many good works, yet all this does not at all avail: he is not sanctified till he believes. But the moment he believes, with or without those fruits, yea, with more or less of this repentance, he is sanctified.—Not in the *same sense*; for this repentance and these fruits are only *remotely* necessary— necessary in order to the continuance of his faith, as well as the increase of it; whereas faith is *immediately* and *directly* necessary to sanctification. It remains, that faith is the only

condition which is *immediately* and *proximately* necessary to sanctification.[35]

I. Christian Perfection and Gradual or Instantaneous

There is an area in which the mature Wesley can be greatly misunderstood. His first writings seem to say Christian perfection is something which by the grace of God is given in an instant. If however, one would be content to go no further one would greatly misunderstand the fullness and complexity of Wesley's thought on this point. In fact, once again, we find a both/and, two concepts seemingly in opposition but which he holds together.

Wesley uses the concept of dying and death to illustrate his point. A man may be dying but we do not say the man is dead until his heart stops beating and he stops breathing. Dying may be a process but there is also a time before and a time after death and death is recorded to happen at a particular time in the Christian sense, when the soul departs the body.

> A man may be dying for some time; yet he does not, properly speaking, die, till the instant the soul is separated from the body; and in that instant he lives the life of eternity. In like manner, he may be dying to sin for some time: yet he is not dead to sin, till sin is separated from his soul; and in that instant he lives the full life of love. And as the change undergone, when the body dies, is of a different kind, and infinitely greater than any we had known before, yea, such as till then it is impossible to conceive; so the change wrought, when the soul dies to sin, is of a different kind, and infinitely greater than any before, and than any can conceive till he experiences it. Yet he still grows in grace, in the knowledge of Christ, in the love and image of God; and will do so, not only till death, but to all eternity.[36]

Wesley also sees sanctification as a process, a process beginning at the point of justification. When one is justified he is at the same time born

---

35   Wesley, *Standard Sermons*, 2:456-7
36   Wesley, *Works*, 11:402

again and at this point the process, long or short, of sanctification leading to Christian perfection or complete sanctification, begins. Wesley sees being born again as being born again by the Spirit and there is a real as well as a relative change which takes place. Such a person is renewed by the power of God and the love of God is felt as well as love for all humanity. It is of such intensity the person experiencing it may be led to believe all sin is gone now and gone forever. Because such a person feels no sin at the time they may easily be led to mistakenly believe there is no sin within them.

However those who go through such an experience find sin, rather than being gone has only been suspended or curtailed for awhile. Then temptations arise and sin returns.

These folks feel the power of Christ and believe in Christ and love God and they are truly children of God. However, they also sometimes feel pride or self-will and even anger or lack of faith. If they continue accepting and following God's grace they are still on the pathway of sanctification or Christian perfection.

> From the time of our being born again, the gradual work of sanctification takes place. We are enabled 'by the Spirit' to 'mortify the deeds of the body,' of our evil nature; and as we are more and more dead to sin, we are more and more alive to God. We go on from grace to grace, while we are careful to 'abstain from all appearance of evil,' and are 'zealous of good works,' as we have opportunity, doing good to all men; while we walk in all His ordinances blameless, therein worshipping Him in spirit and in truth; while we take up our cross, and deny ourselves every pleasure that does not lead us to God.
>
> It is thus that we wait for entire sanctification; for a full salvation from all our sins—from pride, self-will, anger, unbelief; or, as the Apostle expresses it, 'go on unto perfection.' But what is perfection? The word has various senses: here it means perfect love. It is love excluding sin; love filling the heart, taking up the whole capacity of the soul. It is love 'rejoicing evermore, praying without ceasing, in everything giving thanks.' [37]

---

[37] Wesley, *Standard Sermons*, 2:447-8

Thus we have Christian perfection as both instantaneous and gradual. Growth in some but at some point, even if it is just before death, the gift of Christian perfection may be given and received. We can say, then, there is a time before and a time after the gift of Christian perfection is given but the growth or gradual treatment comes after the point of justification and continues even after Christian perfection. In fact there is no place in Christian perfection where growth stops. There is growth before as well as after Christian perfection. Not only is there growth, as we have seen before, one may fall from this high position in the Christian faith and then may grow again.

> Q. 30. Can those who are perfect grow in grace?
> A. Undoubtedly they can; and that not only while they are in the body, but to all eternity.

> Q. 30. Can they fall from it?
> A. I am well assured they can; matter of fact puts this beyond dispute. Formerly we thought, one saved from sin could not fall; now we know the contrary. We are surrounded with instances of those who lately experienced all that I mean by perfection. They had born the fruit of the Spirit, and the witness; but they have now lost both. Neither does any one stand by virtue of anything that is implied in the nature of the state. There is no such height or strength of holiness as it is impossible to fall from. If there be any that cannot fall, this wholly depends on the promise of God.

> Q. 31 Can those who fall from this state recover it?
> A. Why not? We have many instances of this also. Nay, it is an exceeding common thing for persons to lose it more than once, before they are established therein.[38]

Rarely, if ever, does man receive everything at once, justification, new birth and entire sanctification. Normally we work out our salvation by receiving and accepting God's grace and following his will.

---

[38] Wesley, *Works*, 11:426-7

There is indeed an instantaneous, as well as a gradual, work of God in his children; and there wants not, we know, a cloud of witnesses, who have received, in one moment, either a clear sense of the forgiveness of their sins, or the abiding witness of the Holy Spirit. But we do not know a single instance, in any place, of a person's receiving, in one and the same moment, remission of sins, the abiding witness of the Spirit, and a new, a clean heart.[39]

Thus Wesley says there is both instantaneous as well as a gradual working of God in the heart of man.

In an interesting and provocative way Wesley says these who have received the gift of Christian perfection will also grow in perfection throughout eternity. This is a wonderful concept which we seldom hear proclaimed today.

J. CHRISTIAN PERFECTION AND THE SEVEN ADVICES

Written later and published as a separate tract but now placed at the end of his Plain Account of Christian perfection it has some interesting comments for those who have attained Christian perfection and those who teach this wonderful doctrine.

The first advice he gives is to watch and pray to avoid pride. Pride here has to do specifically with being unwilling to learn from others or even more specifically, believing your knowledge is so superior to others you cannot be taught more about Christian perfection.

Wesley wants us to remember the reception of God's grace does not necessarily mean the person who receives the grace at the same time receives an equal or any amount of understanding. There also may be the great understanding in one person but such a person may be lacking in love, which should be man's response to God's grace.

Wesley found some have mistakenly accepted the notion that one who receives God's grace, and especially one who has received an abundance of God's grace, must of necessity have received understanding about God's

---

[39] Wesley, *Works*, 11:380

grace, its reception, and the whole concept or idea of Christian perfection. It is not correct to say just because one understands the concept of Christian perfection they have also received the gift of Christian perfection from God. Neither can you expect everyone who is along the path toward or who has received the gift of God's Christian perfection, has of necessity full understanding of Christian perfection. This would be like saying that just because you can conceive of the creation of the universe that you can actually perform such a creation. Understanding something does not equal ability to perform it or to have received it.

Those who have not realized this unfortunately are prone to or be perceived by others as having pride. This is pride on their way towards Christian perfection or having received Christian perfection, or pride in their understanding of Christian perfection.

> To imagine none can teach you, but those who are themselves saved from sin, is a very great and dangerous mistake. Give not place to it for a moment; it would lead you into a thousand other mistakes and that irrecoverably. No; dominion is not founded in grace, as the madmen of the last age talked. Obey and regard 'them that are over you in the Lord,' and do not think you know better than them. Know their place and your own; always remembering, much love does not imply much light.[40]

The second piece of advice Wesley gives to the professors of Methodism is to beware of another sin which is close to pride and this sin is enthusiasm. Here he is asking them to be very careful about any feelings, impressions, visions, revelations, and so forth, and not immediately and without consideration think they are from God. All of these receipts we have from our senses should be checked by scripture to make sure they truly are from God. There is a great danger when one decides to leave scripture and follow their own thinking or something else. Only the scripture is capable of checking our experiences to see if they are really true. Remember Wesleys emphasis upon the quadrilateral tools for the Christian.

Wesley gives an example of how enthusiasm may creep in and this happens to us when we expect the end without using the proper means. He

---

[40]   Wesley, *Works*, 11:428

gives an example of those people who expect knowledge but are unwilling to search the scriptures and are unlike others who are faithful to God by reading their scriptures to gain their knowledge. This is a great example of enthusiasm. It is also enthusiasm to believe a Christian can expect to be given spiritual strength without praying for it.

Wesley says some believe God writes the scriptures on their hearts so they no longer have to read or hear them. No matter what gifts from God you may receive or think you have received they all pale in comparison to the gift of love. If one seeks or looks for something other than deeper love from God they are seeking or looking for the wrong thing. If one asks another Christian if they have received a gift other than deeper love from God, they are asking and looking for the wrong thing. Seeking any other gift is just not Christian and a misunderstanding of the Christian life.

Wesley concludes this section by writing:

> I say yet again, beware of enthusiasm. Such is, the imagining you have the gift of prophesying, or of discerning spirits, which I do not believe one of you has; no, nor ever had yet. Beware of judging people to be either right or wrong by your own feelings. This is no scriptural way of judging. O keep close to 'the law and to the testimony!'[41]

The third piece of advice Wesley gives is for the professors to avoid antinomianism or the concept of making the law of God useless by placing an overabundance of weight or concern upon faith. Enthusiasm, which we just discussed, may easily lead to an overemphasis upon faith which overlooks the laws of God. Wesley advises to keep a sharp eye out for any movement which tends to move in such an incorrect direction.

> Even that great truth, that 'Christ is the end of the law,' may betray us into it, if we do not consider that he has adopted every point of the moral law, and grafted it into the law of love. Beware of thinking, 'Because I am filled with love, I need not have so much holiness. Because I pray always, therefore I need no set time for private prayer. Because I watch always, therefore I need no particular self-examination.' Let us 'magnify the law,'

---

41   Wesley *Works*, 11:430

> the whole written word, 'and make it honourable.' Let this be
> our voice: 'I prize thy commandments above gold or precious
> stones. O what love have I unto thy law! all the day long is my
> study in it.'[42]

So we see even saying the truth Christ is the end of the law may easily be twisted into what it is not intended to be. We should not forget the truth that love, God's love, in us is shown by our following the moral law because the moral law is indeed the expression of God's love.

Wesley does point to two authors to particularly watch out for, not only because they are antinomian by his precepts but they do contain some truth and are written well. These two authors are Dr. Tobias Crisp and Mr. John Saltmarsh.

The stillness Wesley fights against is the concept those who have faith or even who are just seeking faith and waiting for more of God's graces so as to receive greater faith or love are to do nothing. This stillness understands the proper response is for the person who is seeking to do nothing. Wesley believes God wishes for us to attend to the many means and instruments of God whereby his grace may be remembered and received.

Wesley believes the whole message of God should be taught and though there are times for different parts of it to be taught, we must not be a player of one note, we must play the whole range of the instrument of God—repentance, faith, and holiness.

The Holy Spirit works in our hearts not just for one note but for the full range or orchestra of the graces of God.

So, likewise, the Holy Spirit works the same in our hearts, not merely creating desires after holiness in general, but strongly inclining us to every particular grace, leading us to every individual part of 'whatsoever is lovely.' And this with the greatest propriety: For as 'by works faith is made perfect,' so the completing or destroying the work of faith, and enjoying the favour, or suffering the displeasure, of God, greatly depends on every single act of obedience or disobedience[43].

The fourth advice Wesley gives is to avoid sins of omission. This admonition is once more addressed to the quietists or those who believe in

---

[42] Wesley, *Works*, 11:431
[43] Wesley, *Works*, 11:432

seeking faith or once having faith, they are to remain quiet and not pursue their faith with God. Christians are to seek grace upon grace to grow with Him by being active in working out their salvation together with God.

Again Wesley notes the two types of works. There are those which are directed towards God (works of piety) and those directed towards man (works of mercy). In the acts of mercy we are to remember they are likewise of two kinds, those directed towards the bodily needs of man and those directed towards the spiritual needs of man.

The final part of this advice we would do well to remember today. "Keep at the utmost distance from pious chit-chat, from religious gossiping."[44] These words can and should be written on the hearts of all Christian believers. "Keep at the utmost distance from pious chit-chat, from religious gossiping."

The fifth advice could be taken directly from the title of one of Kierkegaard's books, "The Purity of Heart Is to Will One Thing." The heart is not to be divided but is to seek only one thing and the one thing is God. Christian professors and leaders are to be the examples in this life of living only to God.

The sixth advice is for those leaders to avoid schism. By schism Wesley means "that inward disunion, the members ceasing to have a reciprocal love 'one for another . . . ' This Wesley finds at the heart of what grows into schism. Like Apollo and Paul and the people at Corinth, Wesley says to avoid picking preachers—bragging up some and putting down others. All this type of activity does is to increase the likelihood of problems which lead to schism in the church of Christ.

Wesley then encourages them to attend all meetings of the Methodists and do not think of separating from the others in the bands or societies regardless of whether or not your opinions and theirs agree or disagree. Theological opinions have been discussed previously and more in my earlier book. In fact we are not to believe our opinions are superior to others or they must agree with our opinions. We are to expect others will contradict us and our opinions, regardless of which set of opinions we adopt. To expect anything less or contradictory to this would be foolish and not the Methodist way.

---

44   Wesley, *Works*, 11:432

We are to keep from tempting others to separate from us by trying to avoid giving offense. Speak of God's work as inoffensively as possible. Speak plain and avoid magnificent and pompous words.

If as Wesley says is possible, even a sanctified person can fall and if we do fall we should be honest about it. We should not try to hide it or disguise It. If we are honest and continue to accept God's graces and work with Him for our salvation, we will recover and be brought back.

The seventh piece of advice Wesley gives is long. He uses the sea as a way to describe the fullness of God. Just as all the rivers flow into the sea so does the bodies, souls, and good works of man flow back and return to God.

In an interesting thought, Wesley says one of the best ways we know God's love is by the afflictions we face and God's grace given to us so we can bear them. In a real twist Wesley says:

> The readiest way which God takes to draw a man to himself is, to afflict him in that he loves most, and with good reason; and to cause this affliction to arise from some good action done with a single eye; because nothing can more clearly show him the emptiness of what is most lovely and desirable in the world.[45]

True resignation Wesley says is continually and totally giving us over to the will of God. We are to accept what comes—quickly and without complaints.

The love of God requires patience and from patience comes humility. In fact Wesley says the Christian life is really nothing less than bearing what we receive from other men and suffering their evils in meekness and silence. Because God does nothing except in answer to prayer, another very interesting and exciting idea, we should continually pray for more and more of God's graces.

> God's command to 'pray without ceasing' is founded on the necessity we have of his grace to preserve the life of God in the soul, which can no more subsist one moment without it, than the body can without air.

---

[45] Wesley, *Works*, 11:436

Whether we think of, or speak to, God, whether we act or suffer for him, all is prayer, when we have no other object than his love, and the desire of pleasing him.

All that a Christian does, even in eating and sleeping, is prayer, when it is done in simplicity, according to the order of God, without either adding to or diminishing from it by his own choice.

Prayer continues in the desire of the heart, though the understanding be employed on outward things.

In souls filled with love, the desire to please God is a continual prayer.[46]

Indeed, as Christians we are dependent upon God, moment-by-moment, for his graces which allow us to work with him for our salvation. It is easy, so easy, for us to fall back, to lose our way, to forget the God from whom all these graces flow. As Wesley has shown, all may fall from God's grace no matter what level one has gotten to by the grace of God.

There is no better way to conclude our discussion of Christian perfection than by quoting Wesley when he describes it from three different perspectives. There are not three Christian perfections, there is only one, but it may be understood differently, depending upon your perspective.

I found it in the oracles of God, in the Old and New Testament; when I read them with no other view or desire but to save my own soul. But whosoever this doctrine is, I pray you, what harm is there in it? Look at it again; survey it on every side, and that with the closest attention. In one view, it is purity of intention, dedicating all the life to God. It is the giving God all our heart; it is one desire and design ruling all our tempers. It is the devoting, not a part, but all of soul, body, and substance to God. In another view, it is all the mind which was in Christ, enabling us to walk as Christ walked. It is the circumcision of the heart from all filthiness, all inward as well as outward pollution. It is a renewal of the heart in the whole image of God, the full likeness of Him that created it. In yet another, it is the loving God with all our heart, and our neighbour as ourselves.

---

46 Wesley, *Works*, 11:438

Now take it in which of these views you please, (for there is no material difference,) and this is the whole and sole perfection, as a train of writings prove to a demonstration . . .[47]

Amen and Amen.

---

[47] Wesley, *Works*, 11:444

6

THE CATHOLIC CHURCH

I debated for some time about adding this final chapter. Ultimately the need for Wesley to be understood as an ecumenical thinker overcame any doubts I had of not including it.

There are two sermons which are very clear and to the point. Also, in many comments found throughout his works we find him with just brief thoughts and not a reasoned out or full blown presentation of his thoughts on the church universal.

Those who engaged Wesley at this point were many including members of his Anglican priesthood. Wesley was far ahead of most of them in his ecumenical approach to Christianity.

However, he was certainly not above making short, brief, derogatory comments about some other Christian fellowships and there are an abundance of these short comments. We will spend our time more profitably considering his better and more consistent thoughts.

Even so, the Methodists were started on the basis of a desire to escape the wrath to come and if they were truly seeking it, they were allowed into the fellowship, no matter what Christian fellowship of lack of fellowship they were in.

> But whether ye will hear, or whether ye will forbear, we, by the grace of God, hold on our way; being ourselves still members of the Church of England, as we were from the beginning, but receiving all that love God in every Church, as our brother, and sister, and mother. And in order to their union with us, we require no unity in opinions, or in modes of worship, but barely that they "fear God and work righteousness," as was observed. Now, this is utterly a new thing, unheard of in any other

Christian community. In what Church or congregation beside, throughout the Christian world, can members be admitted upon these terms, without any other conditions? Point any such out, whoever can: I know none in Europe, Asia, Africa, or America! This is the glory of the Methodists and of them alone! They are themselves no particular sect or party; but they receive those, of all parties, who "endeavour to do justly, and love mercy, and walk humbly with their God."[1]

Of course, once in the Methodist fellowship the beliefs and opinions of the Methodists were shared and preached. Differences, if not creating trouble were accepted. Some differences which did create problems of a serious nature were the predestination controversy and obviously the Moravian one.

Wesley could and did tolerate many differences as long as they were not contentious and even then he was hesitant to make any kind of break. This hesitation was discussed in his dealings with the Moravians as well as the Calvinists.

Wesley did have opinions and he held to them and promoted them until and unless he was convinced a different point of view was better. He believed a Christian should hold on to his opinions because this is what a Christian was supposed to do in order to be faithful to his understanding of God.

He did have to clarify his thinking in his war with the Church of England about the definition of the church so he already had done a lot of thinking on the subject. Much of what he said in that chapter about the church is applicable here.

The two sermons which pretty well reflect his mature thinking on the subject are Sermon XXXIII "A Caution against Bigotry" and XXXIV "Catholic Spirit." These two sermons belong together because they discuss the church universal.

It is indeed unusual for one of his day to be so open to others and to seek fellowship with them. Remember, he was an Anglican priest who thought his own church was correct in its doctrine and practice of worship.

---

[1] Wesley, *Works*, 7:281

We also should remember he was being attacked on all sides for almost all of his explanations of doctrine as we have found throughout our study.

Wesley begins his thought by saying there is God and the people of God and then there are those who are opposed to God in some way. Those who are the people of God are those in whom God works with a mighty energy and power. Against God is the god of this world who blinds men to the things of God. The works of the devil are not limited to sinful nations, no, they are found within every nation, even England itself.

God knows those who are his and the devil knows who are his. They cannot be fooled by pious actions or words.

Wesley takes his thought from the question of the disciples who had told Jesus they found someone casting out demons in Jesus' name and they forbid him from doing so because he did not follow them. In referring the case to Jesus he said to forbid them not.

Who exactly is not to be forbidden? Wesley says it could mean that we are discussing a person who is not in connection with us, or one with whom we do not labor together. It could also mean one who is not of our party. It could mean one who differs from us by holding different opinions. Though Christians were at one time of one mind, this age passed pretty quickly relates Wesley. There are a wide variety of opinions now and.

> It is scarce to be imagined he will be of our mind in all points, even of religion. He may very probably think in a different manner from us, even on several subjects of importance; such as the nature and use of the moral law, the eternal decrees of God, the sufficiency and efficacy of His grace, and the perseverance of His children.[2]

Not only could this person differ with us in opinions they could also differ with us in practice. By this he means they may worship differently from us. Maybe even, they follow Calvin or Luther rather than the Church of England. They could likewise even be of another church and even one we may think of as anti-scriptural and even anti-Christian. Those we believe to hold false doctrines and practices could be meant here, too. Finally, it

---

[2]   Wesley, *Standard Sermons*, 2:114

could mean someone so different from us in our judgment or practice we have a hard time loving them as we ought, as a brother in the faith.

All of these could be meant, but since there is nothing in the scripture to clarify whom is meant or to make it force us to accept the opinion that only an extreme case can be meant, Wesley supposes it probably is not the extreme case but rather something closer.

If this person who casts out devils in the name of Christ is not of our party, even congregation or church, if such a person was a sinner and is one no longer and this change in his life came about because of Christian preaching, this man is one whom we should not hinder because he is one of us, he is a Christian brother. We should do nothing to hinder his work; rather we should encourage him in his work. It makes no difference if he is a layman rather than a minister we are to encourage him.

Going back to the early church Wesley says they wanted a man proven before he preached but it was not a proof of passing successfully tests given to them as in school but whether their lives are holy and if they have the gifts necessary to edify the church. If such a person is known by Wesley, even if the Bishops will not ordain him Wesley says he does not dare to stop him from preaching.

> Yea, if you would observe our Lord's direction in its full meaning and extent, then remember His word: 'He that is not for us is against us; and he that gathereth not with Me scattereth': he that gathereth not men into the kingdom of God, assuredly scatters them from it. For there can be no neuter in this war. Every one is either on God's side, or on Satan's. Are you on God's side? Then you will not only not forbid any man that casts out devils, but you will labour, to the uttermost of your power, to forward him in the work. You will readily acknowledge the work of God, and confess the greatness of it. You will remove all difficulties and objections, as far as may be, out of his way. You will strengthen his hands by speaking honourably of him before all men, and avowing the things which you have seen and heard. You will encourage others to attend upon his word, to hear him whom God hath sent. And

you will omit no actual proof of tender love, which God given
you an opportunity of showing him.[3]

Even though we are to love our neighbor and our enemy there is a
special love we have for those who love God. We may be commanded to
love our enemy but we have a very hard time fulfilling this requirement.
There are so many problems with this union in love. We don't all think
alike and we certainly do not practice our faith in the same manner. These
differences tend to divide us apart from one another.

Wesley asks a significant question which is even if these differences
may prevent us from joining all our churches together in one huge body at
this time, why it is not possible for us to still have a union in love for one
another. Wesley answers his own question this way.

> Without all doubt, we may. Herein all the children of God
> may unite, notwithstanding these smaller differences. These
> remaining as they are, they may forward one another in love
> and in good works.[4]

As far as opinions go Wesley says some men may have some very
peculiar ones. It is also a certainty while we know in part and our knowledge
is incomplete all men will not see or agree on all things. For the present
because of our incomplete knowledge and human understanding we will
be of different thoughts about religion.

Even further, we all certainly believe any opinion we have is true yet we
cannot be assured all of our opinions added together are all true. In fact,
we can be certain they are not. Even knowing there must be some errors
in our thinking, we certainly are not able to find which of our opinions
are correct and which are incorrect.

Because this is true the person who is really thinking deeply about
these things will have to allow others to have opinions which differ from
him and they should allow him his opinions also.

> Every wise man, therefore, will allow others the same liberty
> of thinking which he desires they should allow him; and will

---

[3]   Wesley, *Standard Sermons*, 2:122-3
[4]   Wesley, *Standard Sermons*, 2:130

> no more insist on their embracing his opinions, than he would
> have them to insist on his embracing theirs. He bears with
> those who differ from him, and only asks him with whom he
> desires to unite in love that single question, 'Is thy heart right,
> as my heart is with thy heart?'[5]

As to the implications of the question if your heart is right, there are several which Wesley says must be considered. He first asks is your heart right with God? Further, do you believe in the Lord Jesus Christ? Is your energy filled with love? Are you doing not your will but the will of God? Does the love of God fill you with the fear of not wanting to displease God but rather to follow Him? Is your heart focused in love on your neighbor? Further, do you show this love by your works: by doing good to all men and not only to those who return it?

If all these things are right then give me your hand. Notice there is nothing about opinions or worship practices mentioned in this entire list of questions. This is an exceptionally wide welcome to other Christians.

Wesley gives a list of opinions he believes and practices he follows in worship but says no one else is constrained by his particular opinions or practices. If others are not forced to follow Wesley's opinions or practices what does he think they should do?

They are first of all to love him with the love of God which is longsuffering and patient. Also they should not think evil of him. Since they are included in the Christian fellowship this should naturally follow.

They are to commend him to God in their prayers, seeking for God to correct what God finds needing correction, and not what we humans believe needs correcting.

They are then to push and encourage Wesley to love and to good works: help him in the work God has given him to do.

Finally they are to love God not only in word but also in deed and in truth, and so far as we can join together in the work of God.

As Wesley has asked this of the other he expects to give the other the same consideration and help. Though these statements might lead one to think there are no boundaries to opinion or practice, such is not quite the case.

---

5   Wesley, *Standard Sermons*, 2:132-3

A catholic spirit is not an indifference to all opinions because if one followed this line of thought their opinions might change with the wind and they also might actually stray beyond the bounds of Christianity.

The one who has a catholic spirit is fixed as the sun in his judgment concerning the main branches of Christian doctrine. It is true, he is always ready to hear and weigh whatsoever can be offered against his principles; but as this does not show any wavering in his own mind, so neither does it occasion any. He does not halt between two opinions, nor vainly endeavor to blend them into one.

> Observe this, you who know not what spirit ye are of: who call yourselves of a catholic spirit, only because you are of a muddy understanding; because your mind is all in a mist; because you have no settled, consistent principles, but are for jumbling all opinions together. Be convinced, that you have quite missed your way; you know not where you are. You think you are got into the very spirit of Christ; when, in truth, you are nearer the spirit of Antichrist. Go, first, and learn the first elements of the gospel of Christ, and then shall you learn to be of a truly catholic spirit.[6]

Some may think they have broad opinions and believe this is a great achievement. Some are so broad that in fact they are of no opinion since they really don't know where they are. This is not a true catholic spirit.

Just as a catholic spirit is not an indifference to opinion it is also not an indifference to public worship. This person is convinced that their particular manner of worshipping is both scriptural and rational and knows of none other which is more so.

A catholic spirit is likewise not indifference to all congregations. This person is united in one and in this congregation he partakes of all the ordinances of God. In this congregation he receives the supper of the Lord as well as listens to the preaching of the gospel.

Even though such a person is firm in his opinions and to his way of worshipping God and is united in his congregation he still is able to love and embrace the differences he finds in his Christian neighbor.

---

[6]   Wesley, *Standard Sermons*, 2:143

If, then, we take this word in the strictest sense, a man of a catholic spirit is one who, in the manner above-mentioned, gives his hand to all whose hearts are right with his heart: one who knows how to value, and praise God for, all the advantages he enjoys, with regard to the knowledge of the things of God, the true scriptural manner of worshipping Him, and above all, his union with a congregation fearing God and working righteousness: one who, retaining these blessings with the strictest care, keeping them as the apple of his eye, at the same time loves—as friends, as brethren in the Lord, as members of Christ and children of God, as joint partakers now of the present kingdom of God, and fellow heirs of His eternal kingdom—all of whatever opinion or worship, or congregation, who believe in the Lord Jesus Christ; who love God and man; who, rejoicing to please, and fearing to offend God, are careful to abstain from evil, and zealous of good works. He is the man of a truly catholic spirit, who bears all these continually upon his heart; who, having an unspeakable tenderness for their persons, and longing for their welfare, does not cease to commend them to God in prayer, as well as to plead their cause before men; who speaks comfortably to them, and labours, by all his words, to strengthen their hands in God. He assists them to the uttermost of his power in all things, spiritual and temporal. He is ready 'to spend and be spent for them'; yea, to lay down his life for their sake.[7]

Wesley is far ahead of many of us who get so wrapped up in our church or denomination we have no feelings of respect or understanding for those in other churches or denominations.

Many of his insights on opinions and doctrine and the different ways of worshipping are exciting for us today. They point out a breadth of understanding and fellowship which we have not always followed, at least in our local churches. It would be wonderful if Wesley's understanding as found here was continually broadcast by whatever means available through the Methodist Church and hopefully beyond it.

---

[7]   Wesley, *Standard Sermons*, 2:145-6

I find it interesting that in John M. Todd's book "John Wesley and the Catholic Church" he, a Roman Catholic, can write these words at the conclusion.

"The great men and women, like good trees, are good in themselves all through from root to leaf, and use well the soil in which they grow, to produce a good quantity of very good fruit. John Wesley was such a man. A Catholic believes that every man who has followed his conscience will find himself eventually in heaven, with the saints, and able to do God's work, in and through his providence. As I have come to know Wesley I have believed him to be there and have prayed to God through him—not publicly as the Church prays through those declared saints—but privately as I pray for and to those who have been close to me."[8]

---

[8]   Todd, John M., *John Wesley and the Catholic Church*, 192

CONCLUSIONS

We have now taken an intensive look at the theological wars which Wesley fought. Many at the time may not have been perceived the significance of these wars but with the passing of time I think we can see the perception of Wesley that each of these wars was significant for Methodism, and indeed, for the Christian faith. These crucial and key wars are fascinating for us to read about today. Many of them are still issues which the universal church has not yet decided upon, even though they are espoused by some in the Christian community. At this time come comments are in order

1. Wesley is fairly easy to read. He tried to write so he could be understood by others and not write for the 2-5 people who could understand him. He obviously could have chosen the latter because of his scholarly abilities but he selected the option of being understood by large groups of people.

Wesley wrote in the English style of the day. How could we expect him to write any other way? Even reading him in old English he is not difficult to understand. Maybe this had to do with the fact that the writer read the King James Version of the Bible as a youth so most of the language is familiar. To those who have not read the King James Version of the Bible, it might be more difficult. Modern updates of his writings can certainly be helpful but there is something also to be said about reading him in his original words. One gets pretty used to reading these older words and older spellings as well as the English rather than American spellings.

2. One might wish that when he was at war with the words of another he argued in a different manner from the others of the day. Sometimes it is very difficult for us to follow his thought because he uses the form that was being used in his day. By quoting so extensively from the other or often, others, he makes it more difficult for us to follow.

The first thing we are aware of is the duplicating what the other has written and at times sentence by sentence arguing the points to be gained or fought for in the war. This makes some of the reading about a theological war long and sometimes difficult for us to remain excited about.

However when you consider the length of time from then to now, a service is done for us that we would not attain in any other way. For instance, consider the war over original sin. If Wesley had not quoted so extensively from John Taylor's book, we would not know what he was talking about unless we could find a copy of Taylor's book and read it. By the numerous and often extensive quotes found in Wesley, we have a good idea of Taylor's position without having to go to another source.

Another element which makes Wesley readable is that his mind is extremely logical. He seldom strays from the point he is working to make. He does call others to task when they do not write logically, are missing the point, or straying from the point in their presentation. His arguments are well thought out and presented in a straightforward manner

Regardless of all these supposed difficulties, Wesley remains readable and understandable for us today. This does not mean that his thoughts are simple. They are often very complex and somehow able to bring two or more seemingly different understandings of a doctrine or part of a doctrine together. In Wesley, easy to read in no way means simplicity of thought.

3. We should be constantly aware that Wesley is the founder and director of his societies which became the Methodist Church. This was his main work and focus of his attention and mind. He was always on guard to make sure that they were not misled by others in a manner that might hurt their chances for salvation and Christian growth.

Remember the number of sermons he preached and the miles he rode to be able to preach and check on the organization of the Methodist Church.

His focus was constantly on his church. Even the massive number of books he edited for his Church and for others making great books available for the common man is a symptom of his care for those who had put their religious trust in his leadership.

Ever vigilant about what is needed for his societies' health he could not allow them to be hurt and confused by those who presented challenges to what he considered real Christianity and therefore his societies. When their religious health became concerned he went to war for them.

4. Wesley was a prolific writer, editor, and reader. The brother's Wesley wrote or edited about 500 volumes, with John given credit for the bulk of them. It makes one wonder how he had the time for doing anything else. Yet we know of his other activities. Obviously Wesley was well read.

5. It is interesting to me to consider which doctrines Wesley chose to defend. Though I am sure there were some other doctrines of Christianity that somebody was attacking other than those we have considered, he chose these particular doctrines and not others. Perhaps he was not as concerned about these other doctrines for some reason.

One of the doctrines he chose to defend, original sin, was basic Christian doctrine and he kept to a pretty much normal or orthodox position. This doctrine was and is however basic to Christianity and as stated before, a reduction in the opinion one has of original sin and sin requires a reduction in the work God performed through Christ. This doctrine is not one which presented a new or newly raised doctrine to defend against the other opinion. This was a vast misinterpretation and presentation of a basic doctrine which is vital to the Christian faith.

Two of them required a new presentation of an old doctrine but very much updated, changed, and in other words, recreated by Wesley. These two are the doctrine of prevenient grace which was to be used to answer the threat of Calvinism (election and deprivation), and Christian Perfection

Prevenient grace was a satisfactory, nay a necessary and the required antidote to defend against the errors of predestination. By the way Wesley used prevenient grace and his defense of man's free-will he was able to give God all of the credit for salvation but also let man have a choice and a responsibility. He also gave him a necessary way for him to work with God for his own salvation. This doctrine was complimentary with Wesley's concept that man is a part of the priesthood of all believers without using the term. The lack of using the term priesthood of all believers was more than made up for in his concept of holiness, which is man's response and duty to God to serve both God and man.

This led naturally to his doctrine of perfection and fit with his concept of holiness. No matter which of the three definitions you accept, or if you choose to accept all three of them, this totally threw over any idea one may have that Christianity ever thinks about stillness. At least it denies stillness in the way some used it to mean Christians are to remain still and let God do all the work and not use the sacraments and other means of grace. This type of thinking cannot be a realistic position.

Christian perfection is a doctrine we still have trouble with today. I think this is true not because we don't understand it as much as we choose not to understand it. We prefer to be Christian now and then when it is convenient to us rather than always as God wants us to follow and obey him. To Wesley Christian perfection is a goal which we are forever to be striving for and asking God to help us succeed in growing into it.

Wesley shows us that Christianity is not a convenient religion, one that we can put on ourselves on Sunday with our clothes as we prepare to go to our church services. Christianity is a religion of the heart, an orientation for all of life, not just as an occasional outburst of the spirit of Christianity. As a religion of the heart it affects everything we do, because nothing is set apart from God. God is in us at all times or at least he should be, directing, guiding, and helping us grow as Christians.

Christian perfection is a possible goal for us to achieve in our lifetime. It may start at justification but Christian perfection means that one is never to stop growing in love, and even according to Wesley, after our deaths.

The fourth was against the errors of a church. Wesley did not write against the errors of another church by name other than the Moravian Church. One might think to include the Church of England here but I choose not to. Wesley was very close to the Moravians and he learned a lot from them. He even considered working with them in his societies but some of their doctrinal errors became so prominent and created such havoc in the societies he felt he had to go to war with them. This is very sad because they had been so close but were unable to come to acceptable terms of disagreement.

The last is the Church of England which cannot be considered as another church because it was John and Charles' church. It was their mother church and remained their church throughout their lives. The work they did in the societies was created to be a leavening influence in the Church of England but for various reasons finally went beyond that creation. His work within the Church of England had to be confusing at times, almost always frustrating, and forever misunderstood by many.

John loved the Church of England and his doctrines, even those that were most unique to him he says are found within the writings of the church. An emphasis here, and addition there and everywhere the creation of complex presentations of doctrine is the Wesleyan gift.

In considering each and all of these wars the constant is that they in some way attacked his work with his societies and could mislead his church away from what he considered true Christianity. He was their leader and responsible for their religious lives and he would not allow any errant Christian doctrine create problems for those under his care. Like a mother of cubs, when he believed true Christianity, which he taught in his societies, was under attack by a doctrinal error that would create harm in them, he attacked.

5. Some may consider his theology out of date. Many newer books about Christianity and Christian doctrine have been written and we are guilty of somehow thinking "new" is better and more exciting than those written Before. We are also guilty often thinking they are newer and are therefore truer.

I am not aware of any other significant way to combat the doctrine of predestination than by the doctrine of prevenient grace or of effectively making us co-workers with God for our own salvation. All is not gained just because we are repentant and accept Jesus as the Christ. More response and work on our parts is required, always made possible by our acceptance of God's grace.

The condition of man before God has not changed at all, no matter how many newer books are written. God still has acted first and we can, by his grace either accept or reject his loving grace. The response of loving God and our fellow man has not been changed at all. Our responsibility before God and to man has not changed no matter how many more books and emphases of the Christian life there are. In all of these most important ways Wesley is dead on and a writer of extremely keen insight. To miss him is to miss a giant.

Wesley writes at a time in history and in a way possible in history but what he has written is for the ages. We can grow from him, most certainly, but to grow from him we must be aware of him. It is impossible to grow on the shifting sand of trying to follow only the most recent book or books or emphases which rise from time to time.

STUDY GUIDE

SCRIPTURE

Beloved, I am writing you no new commandment, but an old commandment that you have had from the beginning; the old commandment is the word that you have heard. Yet I am writing you a new commandment that is true in him and in you, because the darkness is passing away and the true light is already shining. Whoever says, "I am in the light," while hating a brother or sister, is still in the darkness. Whoever loves a brother or sister lives in the light, and in such a person there is no cause for stumbling. But whoever hates another believer is in the darkness, walks in the darkness, and does not know the way to go, because the darkness has brought on blindness.

I John 2:7-11

PRAYER

O God of Truth, and of Light, my heavenly father, God of the living, lover of mankind, be with me as I begin my study. It is a study of John Wesley but because of who he was and how he thought and lived; it is also a study of your dealings with and love for me. Guide me as I study that your truth may become clear and evident to me. All glory and honor to you, oh God, and thanks. In Jesus' name. Amen.

INTRODUCTION

1. Are conditions so different today that studying Wesley and his theology are out of date and not useful?_____

_____

_____

_____

2. What did Wesley build his theology around? What was the main focus of his theology? Why do you think Wesley focused on these concepts?

_____

_____

_____

_____

3. Where can we find Wesley's theology written so we can study it?

_____

_____

_____

4. What is the difference between a practical theologian and a systematic theologian? Which kind of theologian was Wesley? Why do you think Wesley was the style of theologian you have said he was? _____

_____

_____

_____

NOTES

SCRIPTURE

They heard the sound of the Lord God walking in the garden at the time of the evening breeze, and the man and his wife hid themselves from the presence of the Lord God among the trees of the garden. But the Lord God called to the man, and said to him, "Where are you?" He said, "I heard the sound of you in the garden, and I was afraid, because I was naked: and I hid myself." He said, "Who told you that you were naked? Have you eaten from the tree of which I commanded you not to eat?" The man said, "The woman whom you gave to be with me, she gave me fruit from the tree, and I ate. Then the Lord God said to the woman, "What is this that you have done?" The woman said, "The serpent tricked me, and I ate."

GENESIS 3:8-13

PRAYER

Father of our Lord Jesus Christ who has in love sent your Son into the world to redeem and forgive me for my sin, I give you praise and thanksgiving. I am heartily sorry for my sins and the hurt and pain they have caused to others as well as to you. Indeed I have sinned against you. Open my heart to accept your forgiveness I pray in Jesus' Name.

CHAPTER 1. ORIGINAL SIN

1. Since Wesley did not just write a defense of Christianity every time he read a book with which he disagreed, what do you think was so different about Taylor's book which brought Wesley so powerfully into the discussion? _____

_____

_____

2. How do sin and the cross relate to each other? Do they both go up or down in importance together or if one goes up the other goes down? Why do you think the importance of these doctrines work this way?

_____

_____

_____

3. Which of these two doctrines is basic, i.e. which influences the other the most? _____

_____

_____

_____

4. How does Wesley begin his defense against Taylor's deistic interpretation of original sin? What view of original sin does he discuss? _____

_____

_____

_____

5. What is Wesley's quadrilateral method? How does Wesley use it?

_____

_____

_____

6. What are the two sins from which all others flow at least as far as Wesley is concerned? _____

_____

_____

_____

7. Wesley says Adam's sin is different from Eve's. What does he mean? What is the result of Adam's sin? _____

_____

_____

_____

8. Is more and better education the answer to original sin? _____

_____

_____

_____

NOTES

SCRIPTURE

"For God so loved the world that he gave his only Son, so that everyone who believes in him may not perish but may have eternal life.

Indeed, God did not send the Son into the world to condemn the world, but in order that the world might be saved through him. Those who believe in him are not condemned; but those who do not believe are condemned already, because they have not belied in the name of the only Son of God.

JOHN 3:16-18

PRAYER

Heavenly Father, who is merciful, holy, righteous, forgiving, just, and loving, thank you for moving to forgive me when I could not find a way into your presence. The gift of your grace allowing me to accept your love and be restored to the saving relationship with you is so much more than I deserve but I gratefully accept your free gift. Open my heart even fuller to receive greater graces I pray in the name of Christ my Lord and redeemer. Amen.

CHAPTER 2. PREVENIENT GRACE

1. Who or what is natural man? _____
   _____
   _____
   _____

2. What is the image of God? _____
   _____
   _____
   _____

3. Does Wesley believe in the existence of natural man? Why? _____
   _____
   _____
   _____

4. How does Wesley keep away from the twin perils of Pelagianism and predestination? _____

_____

_____

_____

5. What does Wesley mean by man's free will? _____

_____

_____

_____

6. Do we work out our own salvation with God? How do we do it?

_____

_____

_____

7. Can one logically and reasonably believe in predestination but not in reprobation? _____

_____

_____

_____

8. What is the definition or meaning of predestination? _____

_____

_____

_____

9. How does the justice of God relate to the doctrine of reprobation? __

_____

_____

10. How does the love of God relate to the doctrine of reprobation?

_____

_____

_____

11. How does the love of God relate to the doctrine of reprobation?

_____

_____

_____

12. How can God get all the glory for our salvation if we help or work with him? _____

_____

_____

_____

13. Though God is patient and wants to save us all we can choose not to accept his grace. How often can we choose not to accept God's grace and still be saved? _____

_____

_____

_____

14. Wesley finds seven (7) problems with predestination? What are they?

_____

_____

_____

NOTES

SCRIPTURE

From now on, therefore, we regard no one from a human point of view; even though we once knew Christ from a human point of view, we know him no longer in that way. So if anyone is in Christ, there is a new creation: everything old has passed away; see, everything has become new! All this is from God, who reconciled us to himself through Christ, and has given us the ministry of reconciliation; that is, in Christ God was reconciling the world to himself, not counting their trespasses against them, and entrusting the message of reconciliation to us. So we are ambassadors for Christ, since God is making his appeal through us; we entreat you on behalf of Christ, be reconciled to God. For our sake he made him to be sin who knew no sin, so that in him we might become the righteousness of God.

II Corinthians 5:16-21

PRAYER

O God of love I come before you in my sin and ask your wonderful forgiveness. Out of my love for you which is a response to your love for me, open my heart and life to receive more gifts of your grace. Knowing that you desire a response from me may it be as you will. Help me open my life even more fully to your love. In the name of Christ, your Son and my Lord. Amen.

CHAPTER 3. GOOD WORKS, ACTIVE HOLINESS AND MEANS OF GRACE

1. What does Wesley mean by a "weak faith?" _____

_____

_____

_____

2. How does Wesley distinguish between justification and sanctification?

_____

_____

_____

3. What did Molther mean by being "still" as far as the means of grace? What problem(s) did Wesley have with that definition? _____

_____

_____

_____

4. What would be a magical or mechanical view of the means of grace?

_____

_____

_____

5. What are some of the means of grace? _____

_____

_____

_____

6. What is the power behind the means of grace? Or what is the effectiveness of the means of grace? _____

_____

_____

_____

NOTES

SCRIPTURE

For just as the body is one and has many members, and all the members of the body, though many, are one body, so it is with Christ. For in the one Spirit we were all baptized into one body—Jews or Greeks, slaves or free—and we were all made to drink of one spirit.

I CORINTHIANS 12:12-13

PRAYER

Father, who has loved me when I was in sin and certainly was not loveable, I give thanks for your mercy and goodness. I give you thanks that I can gather together with others who are like minded and share my love for you with others as well as my responses to your love in my life. These members who love you and follow you are precious to me and I pray for them that they might receive grace upon grace. Bless the time we have together with the gift of the Holy Spirit. This I ask in the name of Christ. Amen.

CHAPTER 4. CHURCH OF ENGLAND

1. What are some of the practices of the Methodists (John, Charles, and Whitfield) with which many of the clergy of the Church of England disagreed? _____

    _____

    _____

    _____

2. Why did John and Charles not have a church they had to serve in the Church of England? _____

    _____

    _____

    _____

3. What differences did John and Whitefield have in their preaching and the way they responded in writing to their adversaries? _____

    _____

_____

_____

4. Why did the Wesley's resort to field preaching? _____

    _____

    _____

    _____

5. What prompted Wesley to use the classes and bands in his societies
    and how did he use them? _____

    _____

    _____

    _____

6. What were the two main definitions of the church and which one did
    Wesley follow? _____

    _____

    _____

    _____

7. What does Wesley think about the catholic (universal) church? _____

    _____

    _____

    _____

8. Why did giving the Lord's Supper (communion) become such a
    problem for Wesley? _____

    _____

    _____

    _____

NOTES

SCRIPTURE

God is love, and those who abide in love abide in God, and God abides in them. Love has been perfected among us in this: that we may have boldness on the day of judgment, because as he is, so are we in this world. There is no fear in love, but perfect love casts out fear; for fear has to do with punishment, and whoever fears has not reached perfection in love. We love because he first loved us. Those who say, "I love God," and hate their brothers or sisters, are liars; for those who do not love a brother or sister whom they have seen, cannot love God whom they have not seen. The commandment we have from him is this: those who love God must love their brothers and sisters also.

I John 4:16b-21

PRAYER

Our Heavenly Father who is perfect in love and who wants nothing so much as for me to grow in the Christian life so I may be perfected in love, hear my prayer. Lead me to understand, grasp, and then open my heart to a complete love of you and my fellow man. May I have the mind that was in Christ and the image of God restored in my life and I will ask that the glory all be yours. In Christ's Name. Amen.

CHAPTER 5. CHRISTIAN PERFECTION

1. What three (3) books does Wesley say influenced his thinking about Christian Perfection? _____

   _____

   _____

   _____

2. Wesley thought that Christian Perfection could be described in three ways. What are they? _____

   _____

   _____

   _____

3. How do Christian Perfection and justification by faith relate? _____

_____

_____

_____

4. What part does repentance play in Christian Perfection? _____

_____

_____

_____

5. How do Christian Perfection and the new birth fit or relate to one another? _____

_____

_____

_____

6. What part does assurance play in relation to Christian Perfection? __

_____

_____

_____

7. How does faith relate to Christian Perfection? _____

_____

_____

_____

8. What is the moral law and how does it relate to Christian Perfection?

_____

_____

_____

9. In Christian Perfection is there any sin? How do these two concepts relate to each other? _____

_____

_____

_____

10. How does the concept of works relate to Christian Perfection? _____

_____

_____

_____

11. Is Christian Perfection gradual or instantaneous? _____

_____

_____

_____

12. What advice does Wesley give for those who have attained Christian Perfection and those teaching it? _____

_____

_____

_____

NOTES

SCRIPTURE

The gifts he gave were that some would be apostles, some prophets, some evangelists, some pastors and teachers, to equip the saints for the work of ministry, for building up the body of Christ, until all of us come to the unity of the faith and of the knowledge of the Son of God, to maturity, to the measure of the full stature of Christ. We must no longer be children, tossed to and fro and blown about by every wind of doctrine, by people's trickery, by their craftiness in deceitful scheming. But speaking the truth in love, we must grow up in every way into him who is the head, into Christ, from whom the whole body, joined and knit together by every ligament with which it is equipped, as each part is working properly, promotes the body's growth in building itself up in love.

EPHESIANS 4:11-16

PRAYER

Heavenly Father who has called us into fellowship with you I give you thanks for that call and all who have answered that call. Unfortunately here on this earth we are separated by differences of opinion and differences of practices. May we find ways to overcome these things that separate us, even if we keep these differing opinions and practices so we may cooperate in the work you have given to us on this earth. In the name of Christ. Amen.

CHAPTER 6. CATHOLIC CHURCH

1. Upon what basis were people allowed into the Methodist Church, or Societies? _____
   _____
   _____
   _____

2. What did Wesley say the early church required of a person before they were allowed to preach? _____
   _____
   _____
   _____

3. What is the difference between opinions and practices? _____

_____

_____

_____

4. How should we treat Christians who have different opinions than we do? How should they treat us? _____

_____

_____

_____

5. Does a catholic spirit mean we should or ought to be indifferent about different opinions? _____

_____

_____

_____

6. Does a catholic spirit mean we should or ought to be indifferent to different congregations? _____

_____

_____

_____

NOTES

STUDY BOOK ANSWERS

INTRODUCTION

1. It is certain that social, economic, political, scientific, and many other conditions are different now than they were in Wesley's day. However, in the area of religion, at least for Christianity, nothing has changed. Man is still separated from God, God still makes the first move to man, God still loves man and continues to send his Son into our hearts. God still acts and we react.

2. Wesley built his theology around the order of salvation. His emphasis was upon getting people to know and love God and to then act upon this belief. He was responsible as the religious guide for those who were in his societies and his concern was for what they needed to know and do in order to be saved.

3. Wesley's theology is primarily found in his Sermons, Works and Notes on the Bible, particularly the New Testament. Some material is found in his Letters and even in his Journals.

4. A systematic theologian writes theology to form a system. The effort is to prepare a complete system of the Christian faith in which all of the parts logically fit together. Naturally no system is perfect, capable of gathering everything together as if man were capable of knowing God fully and were capable of explaining everything. None the less, the systematic theologian tries to put everything together as well as possible.

   The practical theologian such as Wesley does not aim to put the total thought of Christianity together. The concern of the practical theologian is to describe as best possible those areas of Christian thought that are of intense interest to him. In Wesley's case his focus was the order of salvation and the reason for this focus was his concern for the members of his society and their needs.

CHAPTER 1. ORIGINAL SIN

1. Probably Wesley's response came because the book by Taylor enjoyed immense popularity even in the schools preparing men for the ministry. If the book had enjoyed only a small response Wesley may not have bothered to write against it. The popularity of the book along with the dangerous deistic errors created the situation requiring Wesley's response.

2. If the cross is God's answer to sin the importance of sin is vital. If sin is of very little importance because man is so close to God the cross is reduced in significance. If sin makes it impossible for men to rectify the situation and which requires the first move to be from God in order to restore the relationship and if that restoral is made possible by the cross, the cross has gained in importance. We see, then, that God's work through his Son in the cross and sin are bound together. The more theologically significant sin is the more theologically significant God's response of the cross. If sin is reduced to just a small error on man's part, God's response of the cross is likewise reduced. They cannot be separated in significance. Any change in significance in one creates a change in significance for the other.

3. Of the two doctrines the doctrine of sin is basic because the importance of the cross is determined from the importance of sin. By "importance" here we mean its significance in the relationship between man and God.

4. Wesley begins his defense of the doctrine of original sin by showing that sin has been a constant in the life of man as far back as we can go and up to modern days. He talks about sin as an infection which affects the entirety of mankind.

   Wesley is pretty orthodox in his concept of original sin and is very close to Calvin on this point.

5. Wesley's quadrilateral method is a group of tools which should be used to understand Christianity and the Christian life. Quad means four so there are four tools the Christian should use. These four tools are Christian tradition, scriptures, reason, and experience. He starts with scripture, the Christian's basic tool, and tries to understand it by the clear meaning of the words. When unclear he uses prayer, then reads to

find out what Christian tradition has to say and uses reason to interpret what he has found. He looks to see if Christian experience follows the understanding he has achieved through his efforts.

6. Pride and self-will are the two sins from which all other sins arise. These two sins infect all mankind leading us to all kinds of other sins.

7. In the Garden of Eden episode we find Eve listening to the serpents lies and she was deceived by the serpent, choosing its lies over God's direction. Adam knew it was wrong but he rebelled anyway and chose to go against God's will. Though they both sinned by not following God's word, you could say Adam's sin was worse because he knew better but went ahead anyway. As a result of their sins the image of God was shattered and twisted and the moral part of the image of God was totally lost—the intimate connection between them and God. The results were death (spiritual and physical), pain in childbirth, and toil in making a living.

8. Better education is not the answer to sin. If that were true we would be so much better today than we were years ago. Fortunately we have learned more in science, health, biology, agriculture, geology, etc. but our relationship with God and man has little to do with education. Sin remains the same and the results of sin also remain the same.

CHAPTER 2. PREVENIENT GRACE

1. The natural man as described by Wesley is man caught in original sin, apart from God, with no relationship with God. He is like one asleep, unaware that something is wrong and he is apart from God. He assumes everything is fine because he does not know better and has no senses to receive any stimuli from God to inform him of his separation from God. There is absolutely no contact with God for the natural man as the image of God is completely gone, at least the moral part.

2. The image of God which is in man is comprised of three elements. The natural part of the image refers to our being created as immortal and were given freedom of the will. The political part of the image of God means that we were given power and control over the earth. These two

portions of the image have been twisted and distorted. The third part of the image of God is the moral image and this part is righteousness and holiness. This part of the image has been utterly destroyed.

3. Wesley does not believe in the existence of the natural man. Natural man is a concept of what condition man is in after the fall without any change in the relationship or action on the part of God. However, God has acted and his action is his prevenient grace given to all. Since all have been given this grace of God, natural man as described cannot exist.

4. The doctrine of Pelagianism is that there is no original sin. Because there is no original sin man is capable to choose correctly and because of this he can remain sinless. The doctrine of predestination concludes that man has no choice but to be a sinner. However, God determined from the beginning those who were going to be saved (the elect) and consequently those who weren't (the reprobated).

5. Free will is a religious term used by Wesley to mean that God has given man the power to respond to God's prevenient or any other grace or to refuse to accept that grace. It does not mean that man can do anything or should do anything and everything is all right or possible. Free will in this discussion means the power of man's choice for or against God, which power God has given to man.

6. Working out our own salvation with God does not mean that we can just do what we want and ask God to bless it. It means we accept God's grace and open our lives to receive His grace and follow His guidance. Salvation is not something God does for us without effort on our part. He is always ready and wants us to accept his grace but he will not force it on us. We are to open our hearts, accept God's grace, and follow his will for our lives. This is working out our own salvation.

7. Wesley says no. If you accept either you must accept both. If you say that some are eternally saved from the foundation of the world, then what about the others? Evidently they are not saved from the foundation of the world. John Calvin and others who believe in election also believe in reprobation.

8. The definition of predestination is God from before the creation determined who would be saved and who would not be saved. This decree is fixed and unchangeable. In a sense no matter what one does

it will not change the determination. Of course those who believe they are elected or want to be one of the elect may act in a certain way. This way may, or should be, different than they might act if they did not believe they were among the elect.

9. If God is a just God how could he do something we would think was bad or horrible behavior for a human being to do? One who rescued two people from a boat wreck and who said they could rescue the other three but chose to save only two would be held up to ridicule and much worse.

    How can God's justice go along with the concept He determined the reprobates would not be saved and then judge them because they did not accept Him—when they could not accept Him because He would not allow it? It does not make sense that God's justice is agreeable with reprobation.

10. How can God's love be shown by bringing many people into the world so they can die apart from him? How can you love someone only so you can force this person to die apart from your love? God's love can send rain and shine upon the just and the unjust. If this be true, how can one say he loves those he has chosen to never be given the grace or opportunity to respond to him?

11. Free will according to Wesley is not a natural gift or something which we naturally have. Free will is a gift of God which allows us to respond to the gift of his grace. God offers his grace which allows us to journey with him as well as gives us the ability to accept his grace and grow with him or to turn our backs on him and reject his love.

12. Some think this is impossible. They think if man is involved in his own salvation this takes away from God's glory. Wesley does not. His point is if it is God's total work by not allowing some men to say anything but yes and some to say anything but no—where is the glory in this? If man has no more to do with it than a rock or machine where is the glory? Wesley believes God gives us the ability to say yes or no to his prevenient and other graces and if a man does say yes and works with God for his salvation it is all God's glory. God offered his grace, man accepted and they worked together. The man could have said no but chose yes to the glory of God. All is God's glory because he offered first and allowed us to accept.

13. I think we can say on this point Wesley believes we can be with God and sin and return to God through repentance again and again. Wesley would grieve we would sin again and again but God's love will forgive us if we truly repent and are sorry for our sins and accept God's loving grace again and grow with him. We are not to keep sinning so God can forgive because we are striving to work out our own salvation with God.

14. The first is if predestination be true what is the necessity of preaching? What in the world can preaching accomplish?

    The second thing is it destroys the need for holiness which is the goal of a life with God.

    The third is joy and comfort is lacking.

    The fourth is it limits or obstructs our desire for a holy life.

    The fifth is it limits or does away with the Christian revelation because it's not necessary.

    The sixth is it makes the Christian revelation contradict itself.

    The seventh is it is full of blasphemy.

CHAPTER 3. GOOD WORKS, ACTIVE HOLINESS AND MEANS OF GRACE

1. Some of the Moravians seem to combine justification and sanctification (Christian perfection) and call them faith. Wesley, obviously, separates the two. Not only does Wesley separate them, but he also finds the scriptural account of a weak faith. This is a faith which is still mixed with doubt, or fear that our sins are really not forgiven. This is a faith before the grace of assurance has been given to the Christian.

2. Justification means one has received forgiveness from God. This is God's act. God paid the price for our sin on the cross. When we are justified the process of sanctification begins. When one is justified the root of sin remains—only when one is sanctified or has been given Christian perfection is the root of sin gone. Christian perfection is a further act of God's grace for the Christian. Christian perfection will be discussed in a later chapter.

3. In order to avoid any possible suspicion of salvation by works Molther said one should wait for God's gift of salvation. By this he meant not

to use the means of grace, not to pray, not to go to church, and not to read the scriptures. The concept, as least as far as the means of grace is, if you have faith you don't need them and if you don't have faith you should not use them.

Wesley was a firm believer in actively waiting for the graces of God by using all of the ways and means God has provided.

4. A magical or mechanical view of the means of grace would take God out of the picture. It would be like believing 10 or any other number of uses of the means of grace would get you to a certain level of Christianity and so many other uses of the means of grace would get you to a different level. This would be a mechanical or magical view. In reality God is involved and one cannot force or make him comply with our desires. He has given us grace and is willing to give us more grace but we have to accept grace and the consequences of receiving grace.

5. Wesley is thinking about prayer, reading the scriptures and the Lord's Supper.

6. God is the power behind the means of Grace. He is the one we receive through the means of grace. The means of grace are a way for man to meet God. Because it is a relationship it is not magical or mechanical.

CHAPTER 4. CHURCH OF ENGLAND

1. Some of the practices the Wesley's adopted over time are singing hymns, preaching without a manuscript, extemporary prayer rather than only using those in the Book of Common Prayer, and last but certainly not the least of these outlandish practices was outdoor or field preaching.

2. John was a fellow of Oxford which allowed him to teach and not be tied to any specific church. He was free to go anywhere to preach.

3. It is usually recognized that Whitfield was the more dramatic speaker. Whitfield was also sharper in his criticism of those he opposed. Wesley was more gentlemanly and polite in presenting his differences.

4. At first the Wesley's tried to preach in the pulpits of ministers who would accept them. Eventually there were less pulpits and Whitfield,

who had been preaching in the fields, convinced Wesley to try it. Field preaching offered a new way for Wesley to preach when pulpits were not open to him.

5. Wesley found some folk who were at first excited by his preaching did not continue for long in their interest and they fell away. He created the classes and bands to give the close fellowship and supervision he thought would help solve the problem of "backsliders" and they did help a lot.

6. The first definition of the church is it is a historic institution which is related to the apostolic church by a succession of bishops and customs. The institution of the church, like most institutions, was geared to preserve itself. The priests were those who were to preach, interpret the scriptures, and administer the sacraments.

    The second definition of the church is it is a fellowship of believers who share an experience of God's living and personal presence and who want to find ways of sharing this experience with others.

    With Wesley both are important and he includes both in his thoughts or theology of the church.

7. Wesley fervently believed in the catholic or universal church. He describes this church as one having one Spirit, one hope, one faith, one baptism, and one God and Father of us all. In his definition he does not exclude churches which have different practices or forms of worship, neither does he separate churches by doctrinal opinions. He is very open to these differences.

8. Wesley was a great believer in the Lord's Supper as a means of grace. The Lord's Supper held a very significant place in his thought and his practice. He also believed the sacrament had to be given by a priest which meant he and Charles could give the Lord's Supper as well as any other minister of the Church of England. His people could go to the Church of England for the sacrament but they soon wanted to have the sacrament in their preaching places. He could not provide enough priests to fulfill their desire.

    Also the situation in America was such no one other than Anglican priests could give the sacraments and after the war of Independence there were hardly any priests left.

CHAPTER 5. CHRISTIAN PERFECTION

1. Bishop Taylor's "Rule and Exercises of Holy Living and Dying", Thomas a Kempis' "Christian Pattern," and Law's "Christian Perfection."

2. Purity of intention which is dedicating of our own life to God is the first. The second is having the mind was in Christ which enables us to walk as Christ walked, or the renewal of the heart in the whole image of God. The third is loving God with all our heart and our neighbor as we love ourselves.

3. Justification means your sins are forgiven by God. This covers all our past sins. This is the beginning. Christian perfection begins at this time but normally is not completed at the time of justification. One should grow towards perfection from the time of justification. Wesley often talks of justification and sanctification. In this instance he means sanctification as the process of growth in Christian perfection unless he says complete sanctification which is the same as Christian perfection.

4. Wesley talks of legal repentance which is the repentance as a result of our accepting God's prevenient grace and our becoming aware of our sin. It is considered the gate or start of religion. We become aware of our sin. There is also repentance in the entire Christian life even when one becomes a perfected Christian. This repentance allows us to continue to grow as Christians ever as perfected ones.

5. Justification is the great work God does for us when he forgives our sins. The New Birth is the great work God does in us by reversing our fallen nature. If we were created in the image of God and this image is twisted, distorted and parts of it gone, then by the new birth our original image is restored by God. We are born again into the new life.

6. There are two assurances in Wesley also. The first assurance is one we may receive when we begin the Christian life. This is the assurance our sins are forgiven and we are the children of God. The second assurance is one we may receive when as a perfected Christian. This is an assurance our sins are taken away.

7. We are justified by faith by the grace of God. Faith is the only condition which must be met in order for one to be justified. Justification has

faith as its only condition. In like manner, Christian perfection has faith as its only condition.

8. Like so many other concepts of Wesley's the concept of the law is not singular. The first time we meet the concept of the law it is as a convincer or conviction of our sin. We become aware of how far we are from a holy and righteous God.

    The use of the law in Christian perfection is it prepares us for the further work of God in us. As we grow in the Christian life the law shows us what sin remains in us and we receive the grace to follow the law. Love is the end or goal of every commandment God has given us.

9. We know before we become Christians our lives are full of sin. After justification and as we enter the Christian life with a goal of achieving Christian perfection, Wesley talks about inner and outer sin. Justified Christians do not have outer sin because those who perform outer sins are not children of God. These Christians, justified, will have inner sin. Only the perfected Christian is without these inner sins of evil thoughts, tempers, and sinful thoughts.

    A last possible area of sin in the perfected Christians Wesley does not call sin. An example would be a mistake in practice. The mistake, because it comes from a perfected Christian, is from love. Wesley calls sin a voluntary transgression of a known law. He calls an involuntary transgression of a divine law—known or unknown—as a mistake deriving from the fact we are human and do not know everything.

10. Works enter the discussion of Christianity at several points and there are legitimate debates about works. Wesley is always talking about fruits or works that come out of the Christian life. Works prior to justification are both good and bad. They are not really good works because they come before justification. However, they are needed in the sense that they arise from the repentance which comes before justification. The works coming prior to Christian perfection or entire sanctification are good. They are good because they are the fruit of the Christian life. Works of piety are those directed towards God and works of mercy are those directed toward our fellow man.

11. It is surprising in Wesley's theology we can answer, both? Remember the illustration of death? One may be dying for a long time but there

becomes a point at which the doctors say death has occurred. One may be growing and moving towards Christian perfection but there is a time at which all sin is gone and love reigns. One word here, growth in God's grace does not stop even here because we can grow through eternity.

12. (1) Watch and pray to avoid price
    (2) Beware of the sin of enthusiasm.
    (3) Avoid making the law useless by overstressing faith.
    (4) Avoid sins of omission.
    (5) Do not let your hearts be divided.
    (6) Avoid schism.
    (7) Remember everything returns to God, our bodies, souls, and good works.

CHAPTER 6. CATHOLIC CHURCH

1. All anyone needed to be a member of the Methodist society is to fear God and work righteousness. He offered the societies to those who had other theological opinions as long as they did not create too much confusion as we have seen in an earlier chapter.

2. In the early church they were not required to go to school and pass tests or exams. The elders checked to see if these persons led holy lives and had the gifts which were necessary to edify the church.

3. Opinions refer to theological concepts and practices refer to the way a church worships.

4. We are to love that person with the love of God which is longsuffering and patient. We should likewise commend him to God in our prayers by asking God to correct his thinking in what ways God wants to correct. Finally we are to push such a person to love and do good works. This is how we are to treat others and how they should treat us.

5. No. We are to be sure in our own beliefs. Indifference can easily lead to not knowing what we believe. We should stick with our beliefs but with an open mind so as to be able to change our beliefs if we are persuaded another one is better.

6. No. the same is true in congregations. We have found one which fits our opinions and beliefs as well as our practices and we should remain there unless we are persuaded another is better.

ABOUT THE AUTHOR

J. Robert Ewbank has a B.A. in Psychology with honors from Baker University, Baldwin, Kansas. He has an M.A. in theology from Garrett Evangelical Theological Seminary, in Evanston, Illinois and returned to Garrett to do further work on the theology of John Wesley.

He is a third generation Methodist Minister. His grandfather served small, rural churches in Arkansas and Kansas. His father taught at Philander Smith College, Little Rock, Arkansas and Westminster College, Salt Lake City, Utah.

This is his second book on the theology of John Wesley. The first is "John Wesley, Natural Man, and the 'Isms'" Bob is retired and currently lives in Mobile, Alabama with his wife Betty and is active in his local church, Saint Mark United Methodist Church.

ORIGINAL SOURCES

Burtner, Robert W., and Robert E. Chiles. *A Compend of Wesley's Theology*. New York, NY: Abingdon Press, 1954. There are introductions to each area of Wesley's thought and then quotations are given from Wesley. This is a helpful, short, and interesting volume, especially for those who are new to the study of Wesley.

Wesley, John. *The Christian's Pattern*. Salem, OH: Schmul Publishing Co., 1975. This is John Wesley's extract of *The Imitation of Christ* by Thomas à Kempis.

—. *Explanatory Notes upon the New Testament*. London, England: The Epworth Press, 1954. First published in 1755, it provides valuable comments on the New Testament that any Methodist would find helpful, but you don't have to be a Methodist to appreciate these comments, as they are pretty solid.

—. *The Heart of John Wesley's Journal*. Edited by Percy Livingstone Parker. New York, NY: Methodist Book Concern, 1916? Very readable one volume condensed journal with excellent introductory material. Well worth the read.

—. *The Journal of John Wesley*. Edited by Nehemiah Curnock. A Bicentenary Issue, 8 vols. London, England: The Epworth Press, 1931. This book provides fascinating reading about the daily thoughts and activities of John Wesley.

—. *Letters*. Edited by John Telford. 8 vols., 1st ed. London, England: 1931. The letters make interesting reading on many topics.

—. *Sermons By The Rev. John Wesley: Adapted to the Use of Students by Rev. W. P. Harrison*. Nashville, TN: Publishing House of the Methodist Episcopal Church, South, 1911. This book gives interesting introduction to the sermons of John Wesley. Students of the topic will find it useful.

—. *The Standard Sermons of John Wesley*. Edited by Edwin H. Sugden. 4th annotated ed. London, England: The Epworth Press, 1955. These two

volumes of sermons are excellent reading. Although they are presented
as sermons, many of them were well written presentations of Wesley's
thoughts upon the subject.

—. *Wesley's Hymns.* London, England: John Mason, 1779. Interesting
reading for the various hymns topics and the poetry of both John and
Charles Wesley.

—. *Wesley's Notes on the Bible.* Edited by G. Roger Schoenhals. Grand
Rapids, MI: Francis Asbury Press, 1987. Wesley's multi-volume *Notes
on the Old Testament* is also available but this is a one volume set which
includes portions of Wesley's comments on both the Old and New
Testaments.

—. *The Works of John Wesley.* Edited by Thomas Jackson. 14 vols., 3rd ed.,
Grand Rapids, MI, Zondervan Publishing House, 1958-59. This is
the first complete, unabridged edition in nearly 100 years, reproduced
from the 1872 author4ized edition and it contains an abundance of
John's writings.

Wesley, John, and John Fletcher. *Entire Sanctification: Attainable in this Life.*
Salem, OH: Schmul Publishing Co., date unknown. John Fletcher was
one of John Wesley's preachers and an excellent theologian in his own
right. Even though it is a little difficult to read, this is an interesting
publication about Christian perfection. It is one of the most complete
statements on Christian perfection that I have read. Paragraphs are
numbered and there is a long question and answer section.

SECONDARY SOURCES

The Book of Discipline of the United Methodist Church. Nashville, TN: The
United Methodist Publishing House, 2004. Any recent *Discipline*
will have the theology of the United Methodist Church in them.
Disciplines before the Methodist Church became united will also have
the same theology that was given to the church by John Wesley.

Baines-Griffiths, David, *Wesley the Anglican*, London, Macmillan and Col,
LTD, 1919

Baker, Frank, *John Wesley and the Church of England*, London, Epworth
Press, 1970. This is the best book I have read concerning the topic.

Bryan, John L., *John Wesley The First Methodist*, Washington D.C., General Board of Temperance of The Methodist Church, 1960. Very short and brief, but interesting.

Cadman, S. Parks, *Three Religious Leaders of Oxford*, New York, Macmillan, 1918

Calvin, John, *Calvin's Institutes*, Grand Rapids, Michigan, Wm. B. Eerdmans Publishing Company, 1957. This is an excellent rendition of the Institutes of John Calvin, translated by Henry Beveridge.

____, *A Compend of the Institutes of the Christian Religion*, ed. Hugh Thomson Kerr, Jr., Philadelphia, Presbyterian Board of Christian Education, 1939. This is a helpful book for one trying to get into the theology of John Calvin.

Cannon, William R. *The Theology of John Wesley*. New York, NY: Abingdon Press, 1946. Dr. Cannon gives a very capable and readable theology of John Wesley.

Chappell, E. B., *Studies in the Life of John Wesley*, Nashville, Publishing House, M.E. Church, South, 1914

Chilcote, Paul W., ed. *Wesleyan Tradition: a Paradigm for Renewal*. Nashville, TN: Abingdon Press, 2002. This is a good book, containing worthwhile material, but is not for the timid reader.

____, *Recapturing the Wesleys' Vision*, Downers Grove, Illinois, IVP Academic, 2004. A must book for the serious student of Wesley which presents his both/and elements.

Clark, Dougan, *The Theology of Holiness*, Schmul, 1996

Collins, Kenneth J., and John H. Tyson. *Conversion in the Wesleyan Tradition*. Nashville, TN: Abingdon Press, 2001. This is an interesting book, but difficult for the average layperson to read.

Collins, Kenneth J., *The Scripture Way of Salvation*, Nashville, Abingdon Press, 1997. This is a necessary book for the serious student of Wesley. Accounts for the dynamic or tension which is present in Wesley's theology.

____, *John Wesley: A Theological Journey*, Nashville, Abingdon Press, 2003 An excellent presentation of Wesley's growth in his doctrines.

Daniels, W. H. *The Illustrated History of Methodism in Great Britain and America: From the Days of the Wesleys to the Present Time*. New York, NY: Methodist Book Concern, 1879.

Davey, Cyril. *John Wesley and the Methodists*. Nashville, TN: Abingdon Press, 1985. This is a small book that has lots of excellent pictures. It contains some good information and is very readable.

Eldridge, Charles O. *A Popular Exposition of Methodist Theology*. Salem, OH: Schmul Publishing Co., reprint 1982. Original date unknown. This is a good book that the layperson will find easy to read.

Ewbank, J. Robert, *John Wesley, Natural Man, and the "Isms,"* Eugene, Oregon, Wipf and Stock, 2009. This book discusses Wesley's theological thinking about natural man, heathens, Judaism, deism, Roman Catholicism, Quakerism, and mysticism.

Faulkner, John Alfred, *Wesley as Sociologist, Theologian, Churchman*, New York, The Methodist Book Concern, 1918

Fletcher, John, *John Wesley the Methodist: A Plain Account of His Life and Work*, New York, Eaton & Mains, 1903

Fletcher, William H., *Wesley and His Century: A Study in Spiritual Forces*, New York, Eaton & Mains, 1907

Forsyth, P. T. *The Person and Place of Jesus Christ*. Congregational Union Lecture, 1909. London, England: Whales/Hodder & Stoughton, 1909. Forsyth was able to say things in an excellent manner. It is too bad that most of his books are extremely hard to find.

Gooch, Joan O., *Being a Christian in the Wesleyan Tradition*, Nashville, Discipleship Resources, 2009

Green, Richard, *The Works of John and Charles Wesley: A Biography*, London, Kelly, 1896

Green, Vivian. *John Wesley and Oxford*. Oxford, England: Thomas-Photos, 1979. Avery easy booklet to read, containing many pictures and some information about John when he was at Oxford.

Grudem, Wayne, *Systematic Theology*, Leicester, England, Inter-Varsity Press, 2000. This is an excellent book on systematic theology written from the reformed perspective. The book takes into account other positions as well. A must read for any serious scholar.

Harper, Steve. *John Wesley's Message For Today*. Grand Rapids, MI: Zondervan Publishing House, 1983. This is a very readable, but solid, book for the layperson.

Heitzenrater, Richard P., *The Elusive Mr. Wesley*, 2 vols. Nashville, Abingdon Press, 1984. This is a very able and interesting pursuit of the real John

Wesley, not a Wesley written by those who saw no wrong, no error, no problems with his life or thought nor a Wesley who was stuck with one idea. The presentation is of a very complex person.

Harrington, William Holden, *John Wesley, in Company with High Churchmen*, London, Church Press Co., 1869

Hildebrandt, Franz. *Christianity According to the Wesleys*. London, England: The Epworth Press, 1956. These are the Harris Franklin Rall Lectures of 1954 delivered at Garrett Biblical Institute, Evanston, Illinois. This book contains solid material but remains a readable book.

Holmes, David, *The Wesley Offering: or Wesley and His Times*, Boston, James F. Magee, 1860

Hurst, John Fletcher. *The History of Methodism*. 6 vols., New York, NY: Eaton & Mains, 1902. Undoubtedly out of print, but has some good material in it.

Hyde, A. B. *The Story of Methodism*. Greenfield, MA: Willey & Co., 1887. Probably out of print by now but an interesting book for those who like to read the history.

James, William. *The Varieties of Religious Experience: A Study in Human Nature*. New York, NY: Modern Library, 1994. This is a classic that I am glad to say is still around and may be purchased at many bookstores.

Job, Rueben P. *A Wesleyan Spiritual Reader*. Nashville, TN: Abingdon Press, 1998. A Methodist Bishop uses Wesley as a basis for devotional readings. This is a very readable book with lots of good material. The layperson will have no difficulty with this one.

—. *Three Simple Rules: A Wesleyan Way of Living*. Nashville, TN: Abingdon Press, 2007. Bishop Rueben takes the rules of Wesley and elaborates upon them for the modern reader. This book is worthwhile and is very readable for the layperson.

Kierkegaard, Soren, *The Concept of Dread*, Princeton, Princeton University Press, 1957

Kirlew, Marianne, *The Story of John Wesley*, Norwich, Fletcher & Sons, 1895

Klaiber, Walter, and Manfred Marquardt. *Living Grace: An Outline of United Methodist Theology*. Translated by J. Steven O'Malley and Ulrike R. M. Guthrie. Nashville, TN: Abingdon Press, 2001. Tough sledding to read through this book for a layperson as it is written for those familiar with theology.

Latourette, Kenneth Scott. *A History of Christianity*. New York, NY: Harper & Brothers, 1953. Though a classic and very long, over 1400 pages, it is shorter than many others. Well written.

Lee, Umphrey. *John Wesley and Modern Religion*. Nashville, TN: Cokesbury, 1936. This is a readable book about John Wesley. It is difficult to find but worth the search.

Lindstrom, Harald. *Wesley and Sanctification*. 1950. Reprint, London, England: The Epworth Press, 1956. This is an excellent study on the topic, but perhaps not the easiest for the layperson.

Maddox, Randy L., et al. *Rethinking Wesley's Theology for Contemporary Methodism*. Nashville, TN: Kingswood Books, 1998. Due to the topic it is an interesting book. However it is difficult for the average layperson.

McConnell, Francis J. *John Wesley*. New York, NY: Abingdon Press, 1939. This is a very readable volume about the life of John Wesley and some of his thoughts. Well worth the time an effort to read.

McNeer, May, and Lynd Ward. *John Wesley*. Nashville, TN: Abingdon-Cokesbury Press, 1951. This is a small, very easy to read book that gives some of the history of John.

Meeks, M. Douglas (ed.) *Trinity Community and Power: Mapping trajectories in Wesleyan Theology*, Nashville, Kingswood Books, 2000. This book brings together the thinking of several scholars on the Trinity and our lives. This is an excellent read for the student.

Nagler, Arthur W. *The Church in History*. New York, NY: Abingdon Press, 1929. Worth the read if you can find it.

Neve, J. L. *A History of Christian Thought*. 2 vols. Philadelphia, PA: Muhlenberg Press, 1946. Excellent history that is readable. This book is undoubtedly out of date now.

Norwood, Frederick A. *The Development of Modern Christianity since 1500*. New York, NY: Abingdon Press, 1956. A good, short history that is readable.

Nygren, Anders. *Agape and Eros*. Translated by Philip S. Watson. London, England: S.P.C.K. Press, 1957. An excellent study of these two words that are so basic to Christianity.

Oden, Thomas C., *The Transforming Power of Grace*, Nashville, Abingdon Press, 1993. This is the best exposition of grace that I have ever read. This is a must for anyone interested in the topic.

___, *The Rebirth of Orthodoxy*, San Francisco, Harper, 2003. This is an important book for Christians to read. It covers the proposed necessity of Orthodoxy and its growing interest by Christians.

___, *John Wesley's Scriptural Christianity*, Grand Rapids, Zondervan Publishing House, 1994. Oden has done us a real favor by writing this book which presents John Wesley's theology in order, plus showing us which elements of theology Wesley is expositing for each of his sermons.

___, *Pastoral Theology*, San Francisco, Harper and Row, 1983. This is an excellent book on the theology about the Christian the ministry. It provides a much needed foundation for the understanding of the activities of the minister.

Outler, Albert C. ed, *John Wesley*, New York, Oxford Press, 1964

___, *Theology in the Wesleyan Spirit*, Nashville, Discipleship Resources, 1975

___, *John Wesley's Sermons: An Introduction*, Nashville, Abingdon Press, 1991

Perkins, Barbara, et al. *Benet's Reader's Encyclopedia of American Literature*. New York, NY: HarperCollins Publishers, 1991.

Pike, G. Holden, *John Wesley: The Man and His Mission*, London, The Religious Tract Society, 1904

Pollock, John. *John Wesley*. Wheaton, IL: Victor Books, 1989. This is a very readable and interesting book, mainly about Wesley's life.

Potts, James H., *The Living Thoughts of John Wesley*, New York, Eaton & Mains, 1891

Powell, Samuel M., *A Theology of Christian Spirituality*, Nashville, Abingdon Press, 2005. Gives historical to modern ideas of the necessity of spirituality for the Christian and identifies what goes to make up spirituality. This is a strong book.

Rattenbury, J. Ernest. *The Eucharistic Hymns of John and Charles Wesley*. London, England: The Epworth Press, 1948. This is a very able presentation for those interested in the hymns of the Wesleys, particularly those about Holy Communion.

—. *The Evangelical Doctrines of Charles Wesley's Hymns.* 3rd ed. London, England: The Epworth Press, 1954. An excellent work on the doctrines found within the Wesleyan hymns.

—. *Wesley's Legacy to the World.* London, England: The Epworth Press, 1938. Well done and very organized approach to the topics. It is a readable book for the non scholar.

Reed, Bishop Marshall R., *Achieving Christian Perfection*, Nashville, Methodist Evangelistic Materials, 1962. This is a short book for laypersons on modern thoughts on Christian Perfection. It is unfortunately not nearly as deep as Wesley, but provides some interesting thoughts.

Rupp, E. Gordon and Watson, Philip S., *Luther and Erasmus: Free Will and Salvation*, Philadelphia, Westminster Press, 1969.Thoughtfully and well done translations of the differences between Luther and Erasmus on this point.

Runyon, Theodore, *The New Creation*, Nashville, Abingdon Press, 1998

Russell, Cherman Apt, *Standing in the Light*, New York, Basic Books, 2008

Simon, John S., *John Wesley and the Religious Societies*, London, Epworth Press, 1925

Todd, John M. *John Wesley and the Catholic Church.* London, England: Hodder and Stoughton, 1958. Written by a Catholic, it is an interesting interpretation of John Wesley. Shows how Wesley can be used for the ecumenical work of the church.

The United Methodist Hymnal. Nashville, TN: The United Methodist Publishing House, 1992. Other hymn books have replaced this one.

Tyerman, L., *The Life and Times of the Rev. John Wesley*, M.A., 3 vols., New York, Burt Franklin, 1872. This is an old standard, but modern research has made it somewhat outdated.

Tyson, John R. *Assist Me to Proclaim*, Grand Rapids, William B. Eerdmans Publishing Company, 2007. A wonderful presentation of Charles Wesley's hymns and his relationship with John, as well as how some of the hymns portray their theological and daily problems.

Watkins, W. T. *Out of Aldersgate.* Nashville, TN: Dept. of Education and Promotion, Board of Missions, Methodist Episcopal Church, South, 1937. A good, interesting, if somewhat outdated read.

Watson, Philip S. *The Message of the Wesleys.* Grand Rapids, MI: Zondervan Publishing House, 1984. Has introductory comments by Watson and then quotes Wesley. A good read for the interested layperson.

Watson, Richard. *The Life of the Rev. John Wesley.* Translated and noted by John Emory. New York, NY: B. Waugh & T. Mason, 1832. This obviously is an old book, probably out of print, but it is very readable and well worth the time needed to read it.

Weems, Lovett H. Jr., *John Wesley's Message Today*, Nashville, Abingdon Press, 1982. This Pocket Guide book may be small but it contains a good, solid theological background for the layperson.

Wellman, Sam. *John Wesley, Founder of the Methodist Church.* Uhrichsville, OH: Barbour Publishing Inc., 1997. This book is extremely readable; covers mainly his life but not much of his thought.

The Wesley Orders of Common Prayer. Edited by Edward C. Hobbs. Nashville, TN: Board of Education of the Methodist Church: 1957. This is a useful book for the layperson.

Whedon, Daniel A., *John Wesley's View of Entire Sanctification*, *Wesleyan Methodist Magazine* 85 (1862):1015-20; 1090-93

Williams, Colin W. *John Wesley's Theology Today.* New York, NY: Abingdon Press, 1955. A must read book for one seeking to understand the order of salvation by Wesley. It is also written with an eye to the ecumenical movement.

Wood, Allan W. "Deism." In *Encyclopedia of Religion*, 2nd ed., 2251. Detroit, MI: Macmillan, 2005.

Yrigoyen, Charles Jr., *John Wesley: Holiness of Heart & Life*, Nashville, Abingdon Press, 1996. This is a must book for anyone seriously studying the full Christian life.